SLAM

foreword by **tori amos**

edited by **cecily von ziegesar**

AlloyBooks

Thanks to:

Matt Diamond, Jim Johnson and Sam Gradess for the opportunity;
Susan Kaplow for the vision;
Stefanie Iris Weiss for her hard work;
Nicole Greenblatt, Peter Lopez, Jason Altman, Angie Maximo and Jen Bonnell for their diligence;
Janee Grassi for her nimble fingers;
Vicki Germaise and Patti Conte at Atlantic Records for the love;
Everyone at 17th Steet Productions and Penguin Putnam for making it all happen, and most of all, the Alloy.com community for the inspiration.

ALLOY BOOKS
Published by the Penguin Group
Penguin Putnam Books for Young Readers,
345 Hudson Street, New York, New York 10014, U.S.A.

Published by Puffin Books,
a division of Penguin Putnam Books for Young Readers, 2000

10 9 8 7 6 5 4 3 2 1

Design by Lauren Monchik

Produced by 17th Street Productions,
an Alloy Online, Inc. company
33 West 17th Street
New York, NY 10011

ISBN 0-14-130920-2
Printed in the United States of America

Woke up this morning right out of a dream

Reached for my pen and pad because my mind was

on a rhyme scheme. . . .

—Beastie Boys, from "Flowin' Prose"

introduction

What is Slam?

A poetry slam is like a spoken word boxing match, pitting poet against poet, word against word, round after round. It's a competition and an audience-involving performance. It's a happening that's definitely happening.

In ancient Greece, the bards recited their poems out loud. In the 1950s, the Beat poets ranted at open mics. In the 1960s and 70s, spoken word caught on in music, and poetry became something you could dance to. In the 1980s performance art was everywhere, no matter how hard you tried to avoid it. Slam is the culmination of all of this—as classic as the ancients, as irreverent as the Beats, as funky as any seventies song, and as creative as the weirdest performance art piece.

The poetry slam originated in 1986 at a Chicago bar called the Green Mill Lounge, where a construction worker-turned-poet named Marc Smith got the mic smoking, the poets jumping, and the audience screaming for more. In a slam, each poet is allowed three minutes to perform, and judges are chosen at random from the audience. The competition can get seriously intense. So can the poetry.

The poetry slam has since become a popular phenomenon. A few slam poets have even made it into films and glossy magazines. Never has poetry been this cool. And the fervor isn't letting up. Poets of all ages are mouthing off in hangouts all over the globe, including on the Web. Slam is constantly evolving—Alloy.com took it online, and now we're taking it to another level with this book.

Slam is a showcase of some of the best poems submitted to the Alloy.com Poetry Slam, alongside legendary poems written by legendary poets, slam poems by current slam superstars, and lyrics from songwriters who double as poets. Here also is advice for the budding poet, frustrated artist, or lost dreamer from people who have made a living out of writing and performing.

Slam is meant to inspire, excite, teach, and treat. Cherish it. Keep it in your bag. Take it with you everywhere. Fold down the pages, write in the margins, read it one page at a time. Read it out loud. If you feel inspired, get your thoughts down on paper or into your computer. We all have something worth hearing, and the way you say it is poetry.

BARKER'S OUTLET

foreword

If we could express ourselves another way, we wouldn't be writers. I think we write songs or poems because we don't express ourselves exactly the way we want to in our everyday lives.

When you write, you can be anybody or anything. Nobody controls what your relationship is in a song or who you are. And nobody owns it.

There are things in daily living that hide behind everybody's heart, and that's always fascinated me. I'm always trying to go behind the heart, to that place where the unconscious lives. I don't think it lives in the brain; I think it is behind the heart.

For me, when the songs start to come, they show me different ways of feeling and expressing, often in ways that surprise me. My music always comes in my darkest hour, and the music is always so giving. I have this picture of an endless well somewhere, I don't know where it is—in the star systems out there. And the more that I'm open to the music, the more that it keeps coming.

Sometimes, if you expose your writing to other people, some of them will try to dilute you—give your words or your music a nose job or a little bow tie. But I'm a small vineyard. And I'm not willing to sacrifice the way I make the wine to get into the supermarket. You know what I mean?

Tori Amos
July 2000

HOW TO HAVE

A typical slam is five poets competing in three rounds. One poem per round. The highest cumulative score wins. So . . .

1. You need poets. You cannot have a poetry slam without poets.

2. You need judges. Judges should be chosen at random from the audience. Judges will score each poem on a scale of 0 to 10, 10 being the highest. Decimals are encouraged, because they prevent ties. 30 is the perfect/highest score in slam. Larger slams usually have 5 judges and in calculating the score, the highest and lowest scores are dropped. If you select 3 judges all the scores should count.

3. You need a scorekeeper. Preferably a math major.

4. Poets choose numbers to decide the order. So as not to be unfair to the poet who has to perform first, we sacrifice a poet on the altar of judgely ignorance. This poet is not in the slam. She is called the sacrificial goat. Her purpose is to warm up the judges.

Now, you are ready to slam.

–Felice Belle

YOUR OWN SLAM

How do you win a slam? That's easy. Be yourself. Once you get your raw self on stage, start to shape, mold, and perfect it. 95% of the people who win slams are their poems to the core. And remember: it really isn't about the scores. It's about your voice and your poetry and having a stage to speak from.

—Beau Sia

Q: Where's a good place to hold a slam?

A: Anywhere where you can get a crowd of people comfortably together, preferably with a stage or podium and a sound system. Don't forget refreshments—good food and drink are a surefire way to draw crowds. Slams take place in cafés and coffeehouses, bars, clubs, restaurants, bookstores, churches, town halls, school auditoriums, libraries, or theaters. The best place to have a slam is where people go to hang out anyway. They may not know what's going on when the slam starts, but as soon as they hear the poetry and get caught up in the competition, they'll stick around.

I want to be able to use my hands in

ways I never have before and it to feel other people's

emotions like sandpaper on my tongue . . .

<<Lauren Brown, 15>>

THESE ARE MY ROOTS

EUPHORIA

today I'm filled with such a feeling of greatness and immortality
I must sit on my hands to control them from dancing
I find blinking a hazard
it takes too much time and leaves me in the darkness
when I could be seeing and living the manic colors
everything in me is magnified and exposed
but no one seems to notice
the air caresses my flesh
and my heart beats faster
and my pulse pulses with the concrete rhythm of the song
        permanently playing

in my mind
I want to write everything I have ever felt before in my whole
existence and

paste them on
the walls
I want to dance with such balance and magnificence
that the whole world will want to dance too
I want to sing like the angels
to part my lips and have the loveliness of my song drip out of
the corners of

my mouth
and to echo into everyone's ears and have a piece of my song
glued into their minds
I want to be able to use my hands in ways I never have before
and to feel other people's emotions like sandpaper on my
        tongue . . .
. . . maybe I will

<<LAUREN BROWN, 15>>

Poetry is a way of taking life by the throat. —Robert Frost

Dare to *say* what you call Apple.
This sweetness, which first condenses,
is quietly put down into the taste,

so as to become clear, thin and transparent,
ambiguous, sunny, earthy, familiar—:
oh, experience, feeling, joy—enormous!

—Rainer Maria Rilke,
from "Sonnets to Orpheus"

UNTITLED

Walking mirror, memories
Brought out and
reminisce
I remember, and now I
see
I am past where she is
I was there though
Now a shadow
To me
To be
16

<<N.S. EGLETES, 20>>

SHE WAS A GIRL WHO FOR A RINGING PHONE DROPPED EXACTLY NOTHING. SHE LOOKED AS IF HER PHONE HAD BEEN RINGING CONTINUALLY SINCE SHE HAD REACHED PUBERTY.

—J. D. SALINGER,

FROM *A PERFECT DAY FOR BANANAFISH*

Me and Tiffany / Dressing up pretty / We love to ride, we love to canter —Liz Phair, from "Girls' Room"

MOTHER

My little mom
Sweet cherry,
Honey bear.
So small, but bigger than I could
ever be.
Bigger than that
One boy last week—
"You know the one."
Bigger than China,
Russia, America.
Bigger and so much
stronger

<<KATE KAUFFMAN, 20>>

WRITING TIP

Shop at thrift stores. Write about who used to wear your new/old clothes.

A poem is a naked person. —Bob Dylan, from "Bringing it All Back Home"

sailboats in bathtubs
the water level is getting low down.
water becomes an erotic passage for him.
(he is shaving in the bathroom)

what can i learn from him if he is like my father,
if I'm watching him like i need to learn
how to shave?

me as a cat
crawling, creeping, coming
stealthily up to watch
trying to decide if i should
pounce
i'm trying to decide if i should
give him an ounce, the benefit of the out
the milk in the half-empty pan

the comfort of my broken,
twisting hands, wringing
a damp washcloth
ringing ears
his singing in my ears.

he flexes his chest. he sways his back
he pops a pimple on his face

i saw dust falling,
as he clipped his whiskers
rinsed his razor,
and turned to train on me

with his eyes. we're two of the same kind.

he says "how long have you been there?"
i say
forever.
he says
"I hope you liked what you saw."

—Douglas A. Martin
(first performed at JitteryJoe's,
Athens, Georgia, fall 1996)

Douglas A. Martin

to a friend

Who prop, thou ask'st, in these bad days, my mind?—
He much, the old man, who, clearest-souled of men,
Saw The Wide Prospect, and the Asian Fen,
And Tmolus hill, and Smyrna bay, though blind.

Much he, whose friendship I not long since won,
That halting slave, who in Nicopolis
Taught Arrian, when Vespasian's brutal son
Cleared Rome of what most shamed him. But be his

My special thanks, whose even-balanced soul,
From first youth tested up to extreme old age,
Business could not make dull, nor passion wild;

Who saw life steadily, and saw it whole;
The mellow glory of the Attic stage,
Singer of sweet Colonus, and its child.

— Matthew Arnold

The essence of all beautiful art, all great art, is gratitude. —Friedrich Nietzsche

Sleepovers at Jamie's

Breathing
in the hot summertime air
Staring
up at a crisp yellow moon
Wishing
upon faint morning stars
Letting
the conversation fly free at ease with
Nowhere
to go, just swing and be
Content
With the nightly morn and yourself and
The Girl
beside you, the girl who knows you
Better
than stars know the moon.

<<Mallory Griffith, 14>>

i thought
  she was her
and she is
but sometimes
  she forgets
and i wonder
and wander

—Saul Williams

A PARADOX FRIEND

She's not the kind of girl / Who likes to tell the world / About the way she feels about herself —Garbage, from "The Trick Is to Keep Breathing"

just look at her
and see
one more vision of
whatever you want
that's what she is
your listener, your friend
she'll say what you want
just write it down
hand it over
she'll read it to you
she has no density
she floats on whatever
you have to offer
what if you began to drain yourself?
she can just see herself
spinning in your tornado of elimination
but where would she go
when she reached the end?
where is she now?
she doesn't know you very well
but she's satisfied
you seem a little kinder
than herself
and she knows all of this
is only an illusion
of everything she doesn't understand
. . . everything she doesn't want to learn

<<Kristin Nelsen, 19>>

DOMI GIR

I was never one of those
big legged mamas
brothers was always
wet dreamin' about
and I could
never
understand
why

Every other woman
in my family was
adequately equipped and
fortified
wid
brickhouse figures
of the most
monstrous
proportions

At thirteen
the most I could hope for
was the
occasional
absentminded
comment
about the
size
shape
and exact location
of my
hard nippled/bra-less
breasts/'neath
that/$14.99/Marcy's
special/purple
polyester/ribbed knit

HALTER TOP

NICAN DLES

which I wore
FIVE
out of every seven days
   that summer

But what I
really coveted
were those
extra special/sashayin'/
   double-seaters
my cousin
         Big Gal
   sported   shamelessly

      thirty four
      twenty four
      FORTY FOUR

I'm talkin' depth and width
Weeks passed . . .
and I wuz still waitin'
for the blessed event
of puberty to
inflate particular
body parts

I wanted to know

what it meant to be
trussed up like a turkey
to hear heated sighs from
   my
balcony window
to be taken
eager

wet
like Zake sometimes got
OH YES

Askia Phillips
dope party
was in three days and I
was invited

Well
not exactly invited

me n about 5 other
girls wuz
sittin' on my stoop
satelliting Sepia
(basking in the glow
of her new girl on the block
popularity)

when Babybra Jones
half-stepped
and
shimmied up the block
straight up in her face

Yo
whatsup
Mama Sparkle and
Shine
Right on Be Free Baby Love
Goddamn

I was undone
here
in living color
was the effigy
to whom I had
lit the candles of my
unrequited love
nightly

but I went to Brooklyn Tech

He was strictly Erasmus
Hall
I watched
breathlessly
as he slid his
three by five
graffitied party invitation
into her left palm

Sepia
Goddess
was by some strange twist
of fate
to return home on
Wednesday
two days before the party
it was my stoop so I
naturally
was invited to
serve as proxy
to serve/as sacrificial
lamb/led to social

slaughter/with
no ass
no hips
I was devastated

Until
my best friend
Rosa
hipped me to a sure thing
the one means
by which I could
improve my
deficit
assets. . . .

Dominican Girdles
Pocket Padders
Bootie Boosters

The ones we'd see pictures
of
in the back of Essence
Magazine
which I could not afford

BUT

Two hours before that party
My
Narrow Waist
cinched
by my mother's
Big Black Belt

My
oiled
Soft and Sheen
finely picked
neatly patted
Sister Angela
Afro
standing at
FULL
attention

My
Spindly Legs
teetering on
too small buffalo sandals

My Tiny Drawers
packed
with
every
scrap of fabric
I could find
from my mother's
sewing basket

I stood

before myself in
Rosa's mirror
swaying
my makeshift hips
in ways she'd instructed

Your mysterious mountains I wish to see closer / May I land my kinky machine? —Jimi Hendrix, from "Third Stone from the Sun" a sight

before tonight
unseen in the
streets of Flatbush

a sight

who'd only recently
discovered the meaning
of the term
Feminine Wiles

HEAVY MELLOW (Too Me)

If I wear bells on my toes
beat a ring through my
  nose
bang a tom-tom till crack of
  dawn
upsetting PC politicos
whose idea of the
proper black aesthetic
may not include allusions to
Stephin Fetchit

n

If I play my music LOUD
stomping up a jackhammer
funk-a-licious on a
  religious
observance day

If I
  hook a
spangled nose ring
through my nipple
  wrap a
clashing feathered boa
round my Kangol
  spray my
fresh Puma skips
green and purple
declaring my new aesthetic
heavy mellow

If I sit absentmindedly
Shange-like
legs open in a skirt
'cause that's how I do
my best thinkin'

If my bed's a
stinking cesspool
of well-worn
day-old chicken
of backlash books
of bell hooks
& poems
  from the Nuyorican
If my hair is deadup
straight on one side
and tell-tale
nappy as the day is long
on t'other
If my ears unwittingly

fill with wax
the minute you
whisper you love no other

If I speak too obtusely
splattering my food as my
friends stare on
wonderingly

If I inadvertently
decide
to be
deliberately
unladylike
provocatively
tangibly
free

It does not necessarily
follow
though you
understandably
may not agree
that I am less of a Woman
when I'm enjoyin' more
of me

—Dana Bryant
(first performed at Nuyorican Poets Café,
New York City, summer 1991)

Exuberance is beauty. —William Blake

WRITING TIP

Write about the weather—the weather outside and *inside*.

WHAT IS

First things first. What is poetry? That's too tough a question for someone as dumb as me to answer. I'm a regular guy who carries around my own definitions for things. I don't know what everyone else thinks, but I think poetry is "no rules" and that's as complete as I can get about it. What is good poetry? That's a whole series of books I can't write.

– Beau Sia

Slam poetry is a close relative to more "traditional" poetry. They're like first cousins. Poetry has a dual history: written and oral. Shakespeare's work was written to be read and performed. In a similar way, the best slam poems are masterpieces on the page *and* on the stage.

Slam is relevant. It is off the page and in your face. It is poetry that speaks to who you are, what you feel and the change you hope to create in this life.

–Felice Belle

The slam tests the poet's courage. It takes a lot of guts to get scored in front of strangers and people who probably don't know anything at all about performance or poetry.

Women and people of color have excelled in the slam because audiences admire eloquence and the audacity to be who we are, raw and uncensored, witty and volatile. Marc Smith, who invented the slam, said that the poetry slam was designed not to create *stars,* but to have the poet be a servant to the word.

–Regie Cabico

SLAM POETRY?

The beauty of slam poetry is that it is easily accessible to a much larger audience than most poetry that exists solely on the page. Slam forces a writer to get inside their words and live what they are saying. The danger in slam is when artists perform a little over the top. To me, a piece loses its honesty when it is not a live conversation with the audience. When some artists feel certain pieces agree with an audience better than others, they can become locked into a staged reading of the piece, which should have been retired long ago. Much like any activity, sometimes one drops anchor in a safe harbor.

—Dot Antoniades

Q: What's the difference between slam poetry and performance art?

A: Like performance art, slam poetry is entertaining. It makes you think, and, like all art, it tries to say something meaningful about the human experience. But a slam is a competition, so unlike presenting a set performance art piece, you have to do your best to win! In a slam there's always an element of improvisation. A good slam poet thinks on her feet and delivers straight from the heart.

I saw the angel in the marble and carved until I set him free.

—Michelangelo

KEEPING UP APPEARANCES

mexican restaurant

the taquitos weren't very good tonite
funny, cause i still stuffed my once thin face w/them
i laughed at some jokes
i had a better time than usual
fidel, the owner, the manager, the cook
called me over
i guess i had a high opinion of myself 'cause
i thought for a split second
that maybe he wanted to offer me a job
my family being the long time customers that we were
but no, that would have been too easy
too easy . . .
for me to smile and say that the dinner was great
for me to walk out and look forward to school
tomorrow
too easy
the reality was he was telling me not to put on any
more weight
and that all i needed to do was to find a good diet and
exercise video

over and over, in my head
. . . find a good diet...no more weight . . . no more
strangely, all i could do was smile, try not to cry
i offered some lame excuse as to why i had suddenly
let go of myself
it's my meds, or i'm going through a hard time
i don't remember exactly what i did say, all i knew
was that i had to get the hell out of there.
out of that room where everyone was laughing and
enjoying life
funny concept.
i did finally get outside, but i ended up facing my all
too concerned family
all i could think about was the previous incident
my mom made me tell her
in my bed it hit me
how could i possibly think that
anyone could ever care for me
or think me attractive
when all they could possibly think
as they hold my hand
is how chubby i've gotten or how
they don't really want to go to
that dance
after all.
can i blame them?
yeah i'm ashamed tonite, i probably
won't go to school either.
how can i face them?
<<Desirée Scott, 16>>

everything i do is
judged
and they mostly
get it wrong
but oh well
'cuz the bath-
room mirror has
not budged
—Ani DiFranco,
from "Joyful Girl"

All that I desire to point out is the general principle that Life imitates Art far more than Art imitates Life.
—Oscar Wilde

I won't be made useless
I won't be idle with despair
I will gather myself around my faith
For light does the darkness most fear
My hands are small, I know
But they're not yours, they are my own

— Jewel, from "Hands"

Perfect

I looked in the mirror today
Perfectly groomed
Perfectly dressed
Perfect little smile
I looked at my resume today
Perfectly straight A's
Class President
Head Cheerleader
Perfect little student
I looked at my family today
Perfect parents
Perfect sibling
Big white house
And money to spare
I looked at my disposition today
Perfectly perky
With sugar-coated sweetness
That must make others sick
I looked at myself today
Never satisfied with all I have
Always wanting more
Insecure, searching
Hopeless, broken-hearted
Pretentious, superficial
Obsessed with how
I appear to others
Not as perfect
As one would think
My perfection is only as stable
As the blurry image in the mirror
Of a not-so-perfect girl
Who can't even decipher
The source of her own
Imperfect tears.

<<Katie Jordan, 19>>

Creative minds have always been known to survive any kind of bad training.—Anna Frued

Try to Pretend

He says next to nothing to you
but expects you to welcome his tongue in your mouth
because you are sixteen and he is twenty
his universe is infinite
your's controlled
you stutter out an "excuse me" when he tries to feel you up
his hands are bigger than yours
and you will not win
the feel of a knife in the crook of your neck
for some reason is not surprising
a sign of his victory
and your defeat
you cannot speak any longer
just stare at the cracked vinyl cushion on the couch
and you try to pretend
that you are not there
that your good friend isn't giggling in the next room with a fraternity brother
try to pretend that the paneled walls don't leak sound into their paradise
and wonder why this is happening to you
not that you would wish this on anyone else
a dimmer inside you turns and when suddenly it is dark
your options become clear
perhaps you will die like Marie Antoinette
or choke on a substance that will stick in your throat like wood
you try to pretend that somewhere people don't pity you
that you are strong and
you will endure this pain
(like you always do)

and you do
later, when it is over
he will drop you off at your house
and say thank you as if you have just given him
directions to the movie theater
shake your hand as if you have just won an award
and drive away as if nothing ever happened.

—Cheryl B.
(first performed at Soho Repertory Theater, New York City, summer 1997)

Cheryl B.

Everything becomes a little different as soon as it is spoken out loud. —Hermann Hesse

the dance

What is hidden is more real than what is manifested. —Simone Weil

It pains me
All of what I'll never be
And I work
Day after
Day
For the dance
For a foot
A leg
An aura
A presence
And a balance
There are yet undiscovered turns
Mysterious positions
And old french men that I will never encounter
There is the air thick of rosin and
Sweat
The juice of the art
And all the pain that goes along with it
All of which I can never really be
My feet, clumsy like an untrained blind man
My legs, weak like young tree branches
My presence, unaltering to a room
My dance
The dance
Two of the same, and foreign to each other
Different for all of the reasons
That they hold from me
They'll never say outloud
The reason
For the dance

<<Jeanne Pfeffer,15>>

MILES AND MILES OF PERFECT SKIN
I SWEAR I DO, IF IT RIGHT IN
... OH YOU WERE BORN
SO PRETTY OH SUMMER BABE
—HOLE, FROM "CELEBRITY SKIN"

ALL AMERICAN GIRL

Maybe she's born with it,
no, it's probably just the
Maybelline
Eat less,
lose more.
Thin thighs for
your man
Bleached out bimbos made of sugar & spice &
everything
nice
With just a *pinch* of plastic
Wait a second? Isn't home grown better
than store
bought?
Wake up girlie, this is the
90s,
I like your eyes, where'd you buy
them?
I must say, narcissism has never looked so
good
Supermodels & Covergirls—"... that's what I wanna
be when I grow
up
Mommy"
If Barbie's so popular, why do we hafta buy her
friends?
Am I missing
something here?
The depths of shallowness are endless; being
vacuous a gift.
Oh, and by the way... do you like my hair
better up or down?

<<STEPHANIE JOHNSON, 16>>

Though we travel the world over to find the beautiful, we must carry it with us or we find it not.
—Ralph Waldo Emerson

The Geography of My Body

It has taken years for me to accept
the geography of my body
its deep crevices and fleshy underarms,
its pits and reservoirs and unexpected forests.
After years of pillaging, starving,
and bunching up fat rolls between my stomach,
I finally gave up and said, so be it.
Luckily, I found men who took pleasure
in my rotundness—*look at those thick*
thighs—and used them to gas me
'til I no longer needed their validation.
This body, imperfect and mostly cherished,
mirrors the bones and cheeks of my parents
an inheritance of slanted eyes, sloped shoulders,
small feet, this body that cradles
a hot heart at its center, like the core
of the earth, steaming, unseen, black
star: its most essential part.

—Ishle Park
(first performed at the Bronx Writer's Center,
New York City, fall 1999)

Spring

To what purpose, April, do you return again?
Beauty is not enough.
You can no longer quiet me with the redness
Of little leaves opening stickily.
I know what I know.
The sun is hot on my neck as I observe
The spikes of the crocus.
The smell of the earth is good.
It is apparent that there is no death.
But what does that signify?
Not only under ground are the brains of men
Eaten by maggots.
Life in itself
Is nothing.
An empty cup, a flight of uncarpeted stairs.
It is not enough that yearly, down this hill,
April
Comes like an idiot, babbling and strewing flowers.

—Edna St. Vincent Millay

I took a deep breath and listened to the old brag of my heart. I am, I am, I am. —Sylvia Plath, from *The Bell Jar*

pull over at the seven-eleven

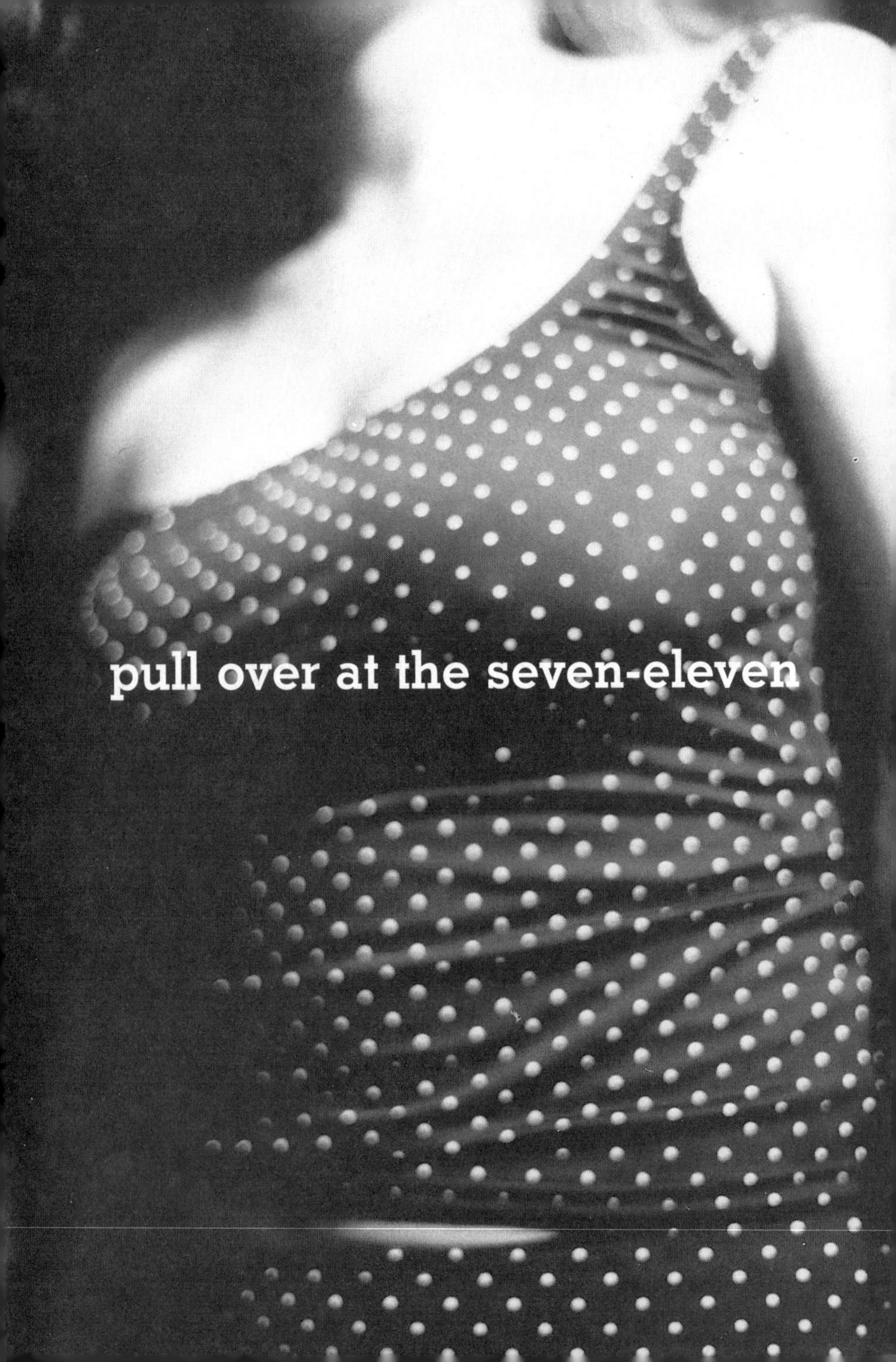

I see the two blonde babies,
wiggling their tiny bodies as they lean over
the mini mart counter,
letting their chests fall out,
out of leopard print tank tops,
and milky white push up bras.
Both hoping to make up for all they have yet
to conquer,
all the things their minds have yet to learn.
And as they scoop up coke bottles
as wet with tiny balls of moisture as
their hair is with banana scented gel,
I just shake my equally blonde head.
For I can see the innocence lost
with every shuffle of a platform sporting foot,
every stride of a pair of shimmering lycra
pants.
And I wonder,
is that how I lost my innocence too?

<<kelly alesso, 17>>

Go to your bosom; / Knock there, and ask your heart what it doth know. —Shakespeare, from *Measure for Measure*

Never insecure until I met you, now I'm in stupid
I used to be so cute to me, just a little bit skinny
Why do I look to all these things, to keep you happy
Maybe get rid of you, and then I'll get back to me (hey)
—TLC, from "Unpretty"

Sea Features

(for Mallory)

She is erect
her bones infused
with the strength
of her imagination

She is waiting
her desires understood
coal burns outside
her new windows

She is returning
her voice found
old fears gone
blood runs to her hands

She is sculpted
her life's angles
cradle her heart
new rhythms beating

She is broad
her skin promising
clasps and warmth
her wrists on my neck

guy wires

keeping me from tumbling

Her shoulder blades
syncopate my palms
and split my life lines
into quatrains

She smiles to herself
and she is warm
and she is rain
and I lean into the weather

relax into her promise
and settle
a few steps closer to myself

—Jerry Quickley
(first performed at The World Stage,
Los Angeles, California, 1999)

Genuine poetry can communicate before it is understood. —T. S. Eliot

WRITING TIP

Sit down with a pen and paper. Don't think, just start writing. No cross outs. Write like you mean it. Don't let your hand stop moving. Go and go and go. Let go. Go deep. Do not retreat.

XIV

Me falta tiempo para celebrar tus cabellos.
Uno por uno debo contarlos y alabarlos:
otros amantes quieren vivir con ciertos ojos,
yo sólo quiero ser tu peluquero.

En Italia te bautizaron Medusa
por la encrespada y alta luz de tu cabellera.
Yo te llamo chascona mia y enmarañada:
mi corazón conoce las puertas de tu pelo.

Cuando tú te extravíes en tus propios cabellos,
no me olvides, acuérdate que te amo,
no me dejes perdido ir sin tu cabellera

por el mundo sombrío de todos los caminos
que sólo tiene sombra, transitorios dolores,
hasta que el sol sube a la torre de tu pelo.

I don't have time enough to celebrate your hair.
One by one I should detail your hairs and praise them.
Other lovers want to live with particular eyes;
I only want to be your stylist.

In Italy they called you *Medusa,*
because of the high bristling light of your hair.
I call you *curly*, *my tangler*;
my heart knows the doorways of your hair.

When you lose your way through your own hair,
do not forget me, remember that I love you.
Don't let me wander lost—without your hair—

through the dark world, webbed by empty
roads with their shadows, their roving sorrows,
till the sun rises, lighting the high tower of your hair.

— Pablo Neruda

This nymph, to the destruction of mankind,
Nourished two locks which graceful hung behind
In equal curls, and well conspired to deck
With shining ringlets the smooth ivory neck.
Love in these labyrinths his slaves detains,
And mighty hearts are held in slender chains.
With hairy springes we the birds betray,
Slight lines of hair surprise the finny prey,
Fair tresses man's imperial race ensnare,
And beauty draws us with a single hair.

— Alexander Pope
from "The Rape of the Lock"

WHY DO

I write poetry when I can't leave something alone. Some image or relationship stays with me and stays with me. Then I start wondering about what led up to that image. And that whole process somehow links up with some previous emotion that I haven't been able to articulate and the whole mess comes out as a poem.

—Jerry Quickley

Writing poetry in high school, I always thought it was something I couldn't take very seriously or go very far with, a little detour with my weird mind and little black book, that I'd forget scribbling once I went off to college. But then in college, things started happening and I needed some place to put them, to help make sense of what I was feeling when the world jarred me. There was my black book. Sometimes things felt even bigger than its binding. That's when a poem would happen, when I had to have some place to put what couldn't be contained, forgotten, swallowed. Sitting through lectures, my class notes would fall off into my poems. I knew there was more to it all than just what I was being taught. There was what I felt, and other things that weren't being addressed. Writing is practicing, teaching yourself, turning to yourself to try and answer for yourself.

—Douglas A. Martin

I write out of a fierce love for the people and places I care deeply about; I want them remembered, I want me remembered. No one else will speak for us if we don't do it ourselves.

—Ishle Park

YOU WRITE?

Q: Do slam poets really make a living doing this?

A: Writing poetry is a labor of love. Poets aren't paid to write or to slam, although there are sometimes cash prizes at slams. And there are always chances to get published, recorded, or filmed, especially at the bigger slam venues. Most slam poets have day jobs. But they make time to write poetry and to slam, because they love it.

Q: Do you have to memorize your poems to compete in slams?

A: No. But the judges will be more impressed if you do. There's an actor inside of every successful slam poet. They love to *perform*.

because we're all looking for the complete definition of love...

—Beau Sia

IT TAKES TWO

I think love is the most beautiful thing
in the world,
and I don't give a fuck,
because I have no original ideas.

I'm a pathetic man
whose goal is to read poetry
in order
to get women
to fall in love with him,
and you'd think I was reprimanding myself
and revealing my horrible dark side
by saying that,
but I was really saying,
"women who hear this, fall in love with me, or else,"
because that's what it comes down to—
an ultimatum,
life or death,
and sure, maybe I'm being extreme,
but *you* walk around and tell me
that things aren't extreme,
jesus,
I've seen a man jack off to a gap window display,
so don't tell me that love isn't important.

and maybe you didn't get that series of lines,
that's OK,
most of them are subtext
designed to impress people
who know too much about art,
all you need to listen to is
the 12 percent
which contain words like "fuck,"
and "ass,"
and "ride my dongstick, you naughty schoolgirl."

because in a poem about love
we all need to know the relevant things,
because we're all looking for the complete definition of love,
if only we could open our encyclopedia brittanicas
and look up love and *know*,
but love isn't that easy.

they say cupid loved *my so called life*
and when the show was cancelled
cupid cried and cried and cried and
decided that he was going to fuck up
all of humanity,
and this is why china has trouble with its birthrate
and arkansas rhymes with date rape
and iraq is iraq,
and the fat lipo-sucked out of california
could be
its own island.

but this isn't a poem about geography,
this is a poem about love,
the bane of my existence,
the reason why I hate valentine's day
and halloween,
which is about ghosts
and I think you know where I'm going here.
I'm going to the land of girlfriends of halloweens past,
and maybe I've only got three ghosts in this land,
but this doesn't mean that they don't bring their friends,
who are the ghosts of girls who have rejected me,
because girls rarely travel alone in this land.
lydia is from this land.

I used to kiss her
while listening to

the cure's "just like heaven,"
now I don't see her anymore,
so that song makes me sad,
why must we associate music with
our love lives?
I'm not trying to be profound here,
I'm just saying that music really takes me
back, way back,
and I can't explain the memory process involved in that,
because I am not a psychology major,
and maybe
my problem with picking up women
has to do with me always asking,
"what's your major?"
but that only makes me as cheesy
as 90 percent of guys
looking for women,
and 86 percent of them have women,
so what's the deal here?
maybe I shouldn't think of women in terms
of picking them up,
and maybe I should open up my sensitive side,
but really,
the sensitive side sucks.
I've been there.
you can only imagine the kinds of sweaters
they make you wear.
it's not fair,
love is not fair,
and war is not fair,
and I don't care what anyone has to say about
any of that,
I feel unloved,
I'm sorry I need people
to tell me I'm cool,

If you wish women to love you, be original. I know a man who used to wear fur hats summer and winter and women fell in love with him. —Anton Chekhov

I'm just that way.
aren't you?
am I the only one?
I know that I can't be that
misunderstood.

but you don't want to
understand me!
you just want to hear the part
where I talk about my small dick again,
because the asian man will always be plagued
by this rumor
until he is brave enough to fling it out
and say,

"HA! WE ARE GIGANTIC!"

this is not the direction
I wanted to take
this poem.
honestly, I just want to be in the arms
of my true love, in a house, in a room,
in a wonderful, perfect world with our
two children,
a boy and a girl,
helga and lamar,
but maybe I shouldn't have said this,
woody allen taught us
that marriage is the death trap.

I'm almost as old as his girlfriend.
she could be the long lost sister
I've been looking for,
maybe my mother gave her away
when we lived in china,

Poetry is an orphan of silence. The words never quite equal the experience behind them. —Charles Simic

wait, I never lived in china.
I think I've begun lying in this poem.
I was hoping to talk about love
for 3.4 minutes
and then
come to a conclusion,
somehow defining love
within the poem,
but
I don't have any answers
and I'm looking for help from anyone,
because love has got me fucked up
and dying,
because I feel retarded without anyone to hold me,
and maybe that's sentimental,
but what's wrong with sentimental?

I just need love—

to self: fuck you, I'm OK!

you see, I can't even decide what I need
much less understand what I'm saying.
you see, all I'm saying
is
someone love me.

—Beau Sia
(first performed at
Marymount Manhattan College,
New York City, fall 1996)

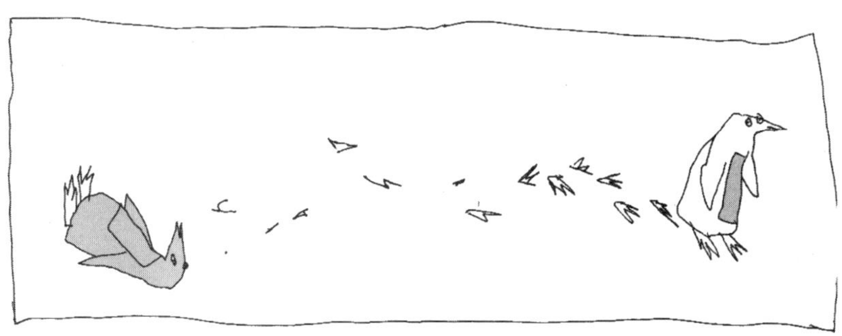
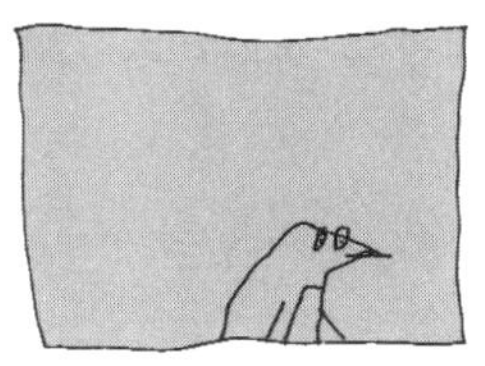

"Penguin"
artwork by Beau Sia

Insecure Anticipations

In the night
we sit
in hushed trepidation
our eyes meet
we look away
you nervously tap the
steering wheel
I habitually flick your lighter
We look for ease in
forced conversations.
Your eyes wander as you talk
and I laugh
at all the wrong times
I yearn to lean on your
  shoulder,
kiss your cheek,
and hold you close

Emotion is the best mnemonic device. —Alice Fulton

But I sit there waiting,
waiting for an automatic comfort
and an instant bond.
I want to tell you my deepest
   secrets,
give you my body, and
tingle with warm love
You yearn for the same
we want so much, yet
hold back even more.
We wait in anticipation on
opposite couches and
avoid any depth
and melt each time we touch,
a courageous move as
fleeting as the comfort of
your eyes.

<<Jeanne Pfeffer, 15>>

WRITING TIP

Think of something you really wish would happen.
Start writing. Anything can happen in a poem.

somewhere i have never travelled, gladly beyond

somewhere i have never travelled,gladly beyond
any experience, your eyes have their silence:
in your most frail gesture are things which enclose me,
or which i cannot touch because they are too near

your slightest look easily will unclose me
though i have closed myself as fingers,
you open always petal by petal myself as Spring opens
(touching skilfully,mysteriously)her first rose

or if your wish be to close me,i and
my life will shut very beautifully,suddenly,
as when the heart of this flower imagines
the snow carefully everywhere descending;

nothing which we are to perceive in this world equals
the power of your intense fragility:whose texture
compels me with the colour of its countries,
rendering death and forever with each breathing

(i do not know what it is about you that closes
and opens;only something in me understands
the voice of your eyes is deeper than all roses)
nobody,not even the rain,has such small hands

—E. E. Cummings

Love is the poetry of the senses. —Honoré de Balzac

Love of Rain

the rain falls on your head

and drops mingle with your dark hair

you've never looked more beautiful to me

hold me in your arms

never let me go

I feel so safe when you're with me

lazily your lips smile

kisses fall soft

<<Missy Parker, 19>>

polarattraction

you are in it

you're driven to be

of their kind

you need the rush

you have the goal

i have the spark

i need the reins

i'm driven to

stand alone

i am subtle

it's simple:

you crave the rage—

and

i crave you.

<<Lynette Muhlestein, 16>>

Poetry is either something that lives like fire inside you— like music to the musician . . .—or else it is nothing, an empty, formalised bore around which pedants can endlessly drone their notes and explanations. —F. Scott Fitzgerald

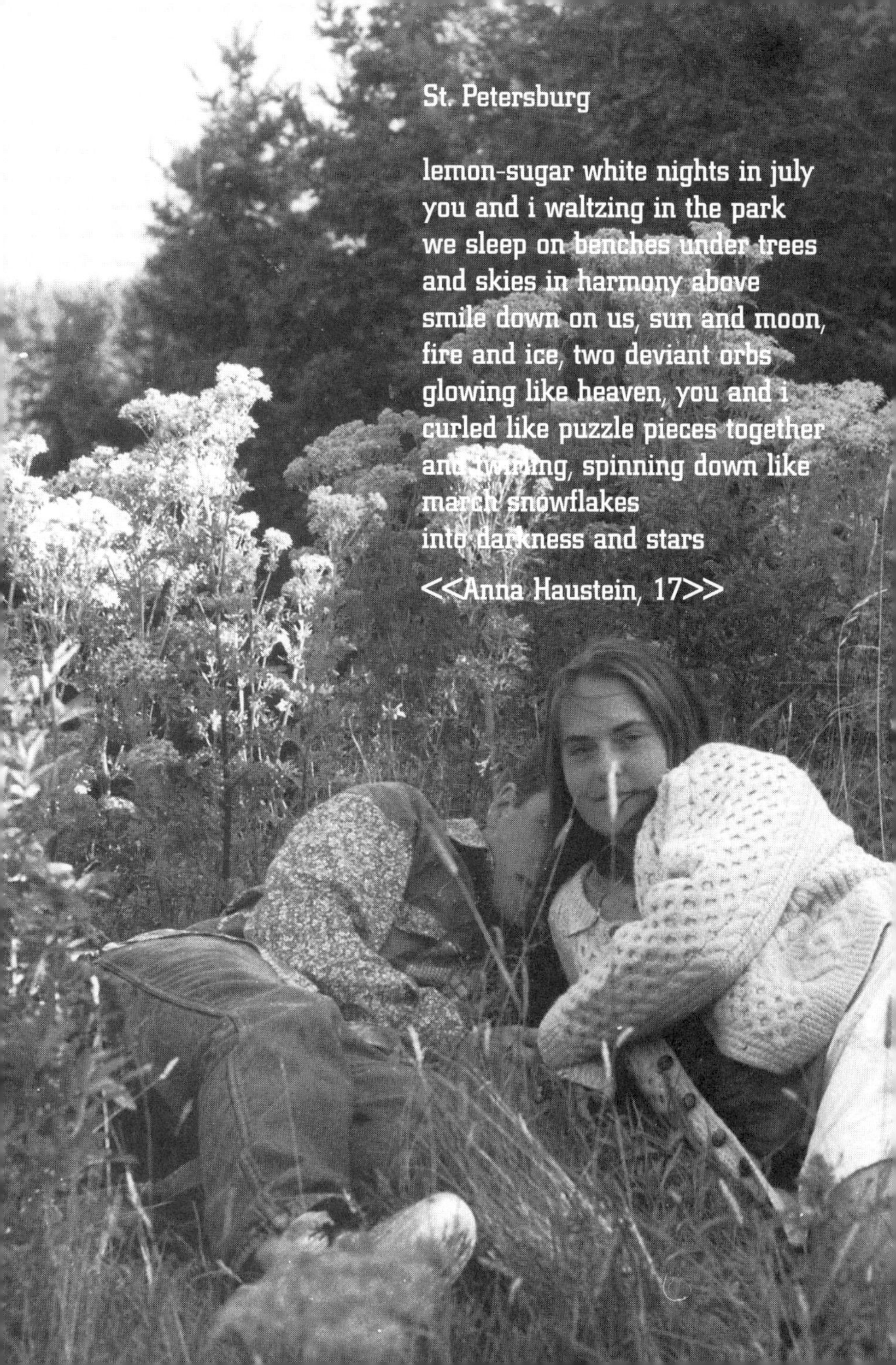

St. Petersburg

lemon-sugar white nights in july
you and i waltzing in the park
we sleep on benches under trees
and skies in harmony above
smile down on us, sun and moon,
fire and ice, two deviant orbs
glowing like heaven, you and i
curled like puzzle pieces together
and twirling, spinning down like
march snowflakes
into darkness and stars

<<Anna Haustein, 17>>

Plugging *The Basketball Diaries* for Leonardo DiCaprio

The thought of your limber body
curved
over the camera
dribbling those Spalding balls
shirtless, Mr. DiCaprio
steams the milk in the depths
of my dark cappuccino

so I turn on the tube hoping to spot you
hung on the naked rim of a hoop
mooning the Circle Line Cruise
or jerking off on the roof

Instead I catch you flashing smiles
for that cross-legged MTV bimba named Daisy

Enamored by your bashfulness,
She leans towards you
like an awkward sunflower
in heat
and asks:

you're the hottest actor right now
which girls are after you

you remain silent–
a femme little thing
in a butch leather jacket

I'm asking about your love life
but you say there's no one

Walking past Tower Records,

I freeze in my tracks at the sight of your stance:

    a savage cheetah with a crimson smile/
    Catholicism's leash
    tied round your virgin neck

You may be too young
to catch my entendres, Nardo

but I'd like to give you
an Oscar

—Regie Cabico
(first performed at Nuyorican Poets Café,
New York City, 1995)

Everything that makes more of you than you have ever been, even in your best hours, is right.
—Rainer Maria Rilke, from *Letters to a Young Poet*

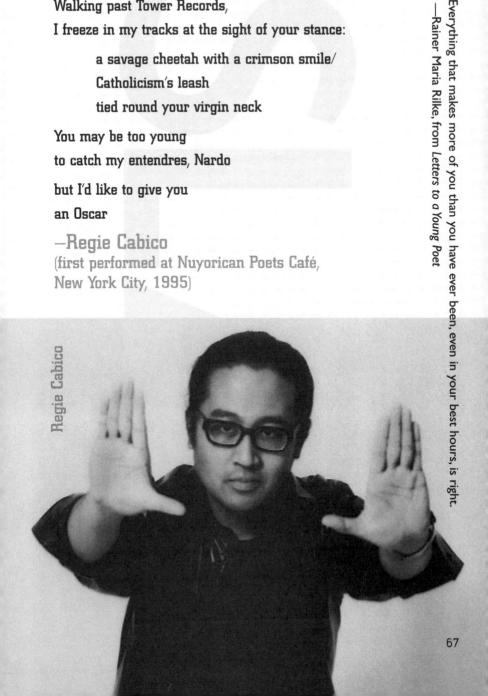

Regie Cabico

A love poem

I'm writing a love poem
Because for that one moment,
Kneeling there at my kitchen table
Peach juice running down your fingers
As you sliced the fruit
I loved you.
You offered me a piece
Held it up for my approval
Laughing as the sticky drops hit the wood
And dripped to the tile floor beneath.
Then you kissed me,
And the moment was over.

<<Jessica Dzaman, 14>>

Wine is bottled poetry. —Robert Louis Stevenson

THIS IS
JUST TO SAY

I have eaten
the plums
that were in
the icebox

and which
you were probably
saving
for breakfast

Forgive me
they were delicious
so sweet
and so cold

—WILLIAM CARLOS WILLIAMS

It's not

just you

it's the idea

of you

the idea of love

to rub my hands

across your back

to kiss you

knowing

what no one else

knows about you

seeing you

at your weakest

moments

because you're

delicate

your smile

your strong hugs

it's the idea of

you

that makes

my

stomach

tingle.

<<Isabella Joy, 18>>

With love one can live even without happiness. —Fyodor Dostoyevsky

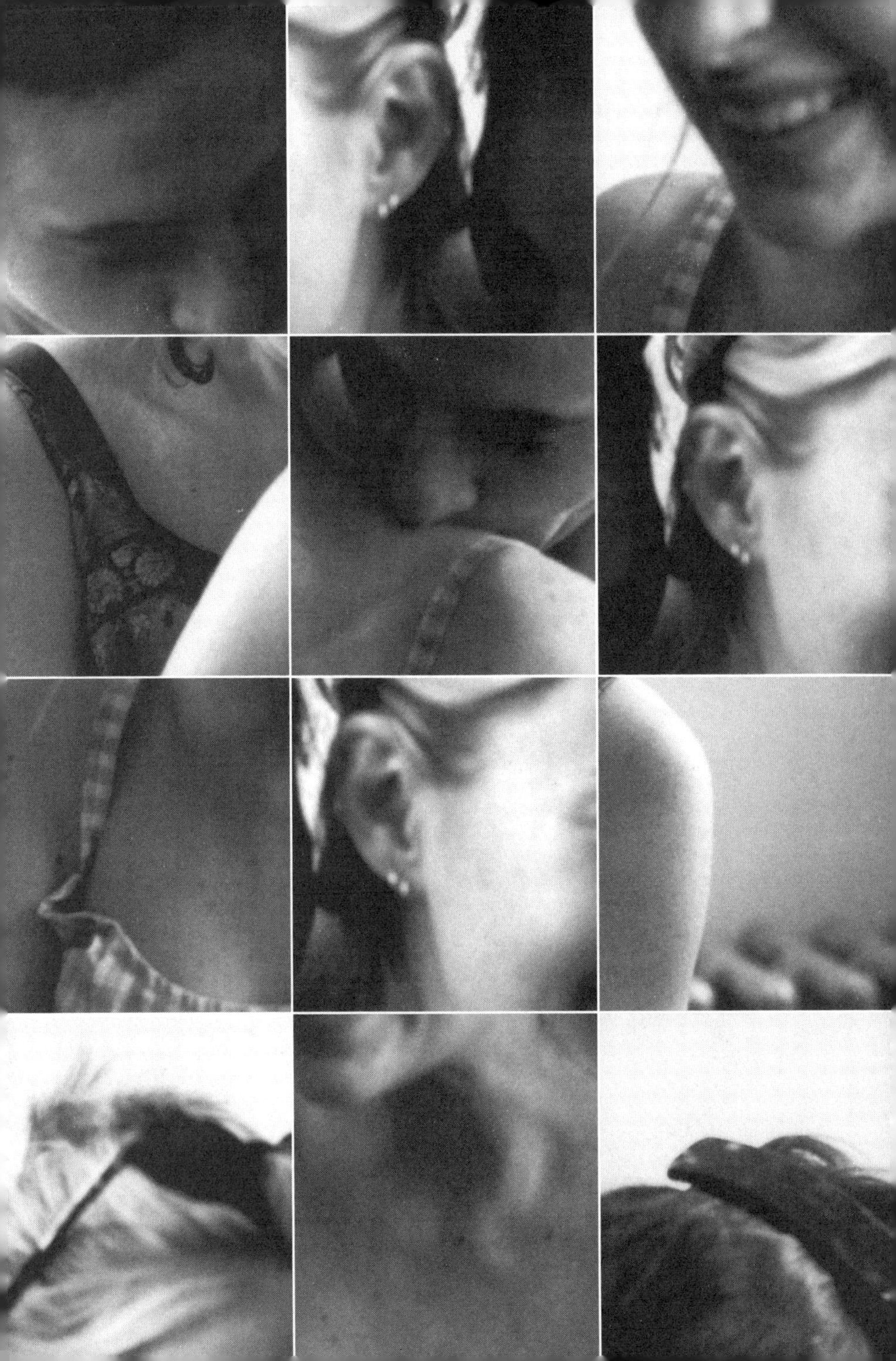

Love Song For the Drummer

He was chocolatemahoganybrownbrickred
several shades of Indian earth blended
no lines
creaseless
Symmetry danced in his veins
my inner sonata silenced
I became 1 movement/fluid
blushing beige at the thought of him in
   his boyhood
palms down
panting the vulnerability out of me
vulgar ability I have
to fantasize myself into his country
without knowing anything except
percussion turns me on
But it wasn't about him/it was the song
La musica beating me ceaseless/senseless

I am young/so young/yet
have old eyes
a stolen soul
I steal souls
but viscerally speaking
my tummy doesn't tumblesaul when I see him
But when I *hear* him
my spirit sambas uncontrollably
as if *La Mariachi*
were plucking steel/string/sinews inside me
Barely breathing
percussion rushing thru me
I could see nothing
I was surrounded by sound
panties stained a deeper shade of clay

as the rhythm made its home between my legs
hatching sunsets
a warmth only I was aware of

His spirit: soft blunted blade
entering through my exit
I thought I had been spade
reinvented *manmade*
Music/I want you to lay
in the soft shell cave of my thighs
fill the echoes
make me come legato
because my poems have been plosive
too macho
Raise me 12 notes higher
sweaty palms ride me bareback
give phoenix her flames back
fan the silent valley under her wings
let her sing
until they cut out her tongue
or/the nightingale gets jealous
Wake Calliope
There's salsa on the glossy cedar dance floor
now that I've drank the last drop I want more

I want to know
how bodies moved
in the first shadow of night
before the lights came on
and we saw
and were shamed
cos we felt so good
for our *own* sake

The important thing is to feel your music, really feel it and believe it. —Ray Charles

I want more musica keeping my shoulders strong
womb thumping birth of bass
immaculate/no blueprint
to the submission into mass movement
I do not want to merely reflect
He was musician
I was nothing but me listening
trying to tear the atmosphere desperately
because gravity distracts me/keeps me from myself
I swore his eyes were not jewels.
They were dark/rich like chocolate
bigger than Guatemala
They knew things I wanted to know

That night I believed/I believed
Religion escaped me
faith became me
Alone
I dropped to knees/humbled/
and samba'd myself to sleep

—Dot Antoniades
(first performed at the Nuyorican Poets Café,
New York City, 1998)

Dot Antoniades

SUPERMAN

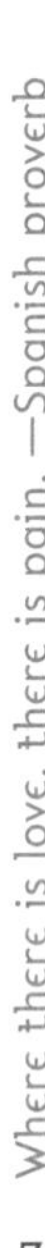

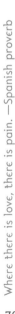

Moths flicker under the golden glow of the street lamps.
Why does it take so much longer to get back home?
There's no reason for me to glance back with innocent smiles.
No sarcastic remarks about me hanging my head out the car window—
Hair glossed to my lips.
Listening to the songs that you should be singing with me.
Sole lyrics. Bouncing through my head.
Vaguely conscious of the buzzing traffic that surrounds me.
Party night—

Nearly seduced,
Skipping the cracks and counting the little yellow
   lines in the street.
24-25-26
If the world falls from beneath me, will you be here to
   save me?
If only I could understand those long silent pauses
   when you aren't singing
along.
I think the world may be falling now . . .
27-28-29

<<KRISTIN DRAKE, 16>>

wildish

I resist the urge to just leave, just flee
see, I see you across the gloom.
Bell-shaped blosoms glittering glossing,
around the tinsled folds of your hems,
folded hands.

Saw-dust on my shoes I sway,
swear under my breath
my upper-lip a bit
of fuzz,
I taste peach
in my mouth

you are beyond the barricades,
I cave in
con-vex, curse
myself sealed in this room full of peers

I head for the way out.
but your song catches me in movement.

I glisten,
in tune I light up
in the forward rush of flux.
Your hands clutch on my shoulders, touch

bolder, I sway
pray simple aligned with you,
and the teether strap of your baying

we stay glued to the spot
light on the floor

the smell of your awe-berry velvet

so very soft and lost
with me and understanding

–Douglas A. Martin
(never performed)

WRITING TIP

Read poetry aloud every chance you get. Don't worry about people thinking you're insane. If you are worried about this, find somewhere private to do it. Learn to love your voice. Read poetry to your boyfriend/girlfriend and ask them to read poetry to you. If you're unattached, fantasize about who you want to read to you.

Reality only reveals itself when it is illuminated by a ray of poetry.

—George Braque

Saul Williams

i lie to you
about twice a day
—Saul Williams

ICE

I sit alone, waiting for him, them,
In the little booth where the two of them and me
Not the three of us,
The two of them and me,
Eat, have eaten, every morning.
A lonely smoke signal issues from one booth.
The smoking crowd isn't here till nine.
His battered pickup goes by,
My normal 8-track mind folds into one.
Anticipation mounts.
I imagine him slamming his door shut,
The tailgate rattles, the mirror falls off. Again.
His Airwalks scuff the leaves forgotten and brown.
The diner's door pulls open, an inch, . . . two,
Then shuts, teasing me, laughing.
He reads the headlines screaming from the machines.
My head faces front, away from him,
Refusing to admit to the world, I'm waiting for him,
But the empty booth in front of me knows.

Take hold lightly, let go lightly. This is one of the great secrets of felicity in love. —Spainish Proverb

It glares garish orange, sharply contrasting my Lysol one.
Finally I hear the door open.
A blast of cold rushes in with the street sounds.
I feel him pause like all outlaws before entering a bar.
Did the room fall silent? Or is the pounding of my heart
Blocking out the world?
I feel him walking towards me, then past my booth,
Limping slightly from an imagined football injury.
He turns once to take me in,
My lemon fresh booth, and forlorn Coke.
That yellow Freshjive shirt I love is masked
By his brother's hideous, green jacket.
Noting my brother's absence he limps purposefully
Toward the counter.
My brother walks to him.
Funny, when had he come in?
They saunter back with four biscuits.
No napkins.
They congratulate each other for being kings.
He runs long fingers through his hair;
It stands on end like a blonde afro.

Our eyes meet, his gorgeous brown eyes,
I think maybe I see a person behind them,
But my brother mentions the game.
He becomes macho again.
His styrafoam cup tips, ice pebbles scatter.
They barely notice.
Sprite races to their laps, so they stand up,
And pause to look at four girls.
I turn my attention back to the ice.
I'm left to clean up his mess.
Someone's always left to clean up his messes.
I could have another guy, yet I wait for
One, just one, to grow up.
But his brothers never did. Will he?
The door is now closed but the November air
Still chills.
I grab my books and walk outside
Leaving the ice still melting
In little puddles on the table.

<<A. L. HERRON, 17>>

Perfect understanding will sometimes almost extinguish pleasure. —A. E. Housman

The Sick Day

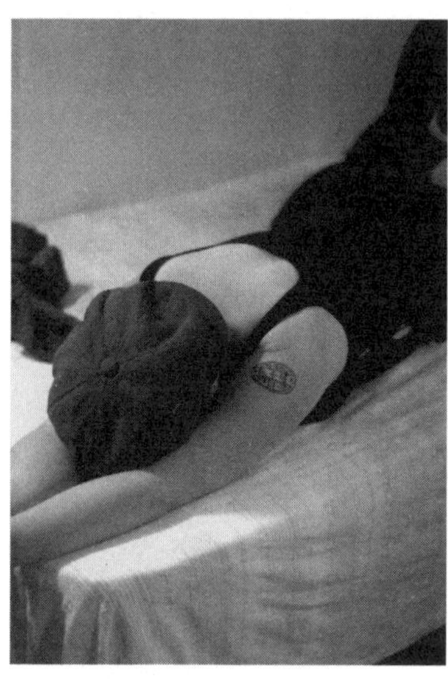

The Friday phone call
The Saturday cookie
and ice cream binge
The Sunday mall therapy
And Monday
The sick day
I lie in the bed
Master bedroom
king-size mattress
In jeans I wore
The weekend straight
Pretending I have the flu
With a soap blaring
And a tissue box nearby
There was no way
I could go to class today
Not as long
as it's your nape
I have to stare at
And when the digital clock
Says school's out
And the bell rings with
the cordless phone buried
under the comforter and
used kleenex
And it's a Monday phone call
From your friend
And I smile
And change my jeans

<<Darcy Porter, 15>>

Strangely Enough

Strangely enough I saw you today
tripping down the street
and I didn't feel so foreign anymore.
My hands became a little smaller and I
didn't need to clasp them so tightly to my side.
My molded grin became real to me
dusting off the cobwebbed corners.

Strangely enough I saw you today
staring hard at me
and I saw a new fancy in myself.
Curves candying my body like a sweet coating,
and I stood a little taller.
Flecks in your eyes caught the sun's sparkles
like a prism in my mind.

Strangely enough I saw you today
You spoke to me like an old friend.
My paperdoll world found a sweet reality
that formed Steinke poetry in my veins.
Your warm hands brushed my shoulder before you left
and the heat traveled through my body
like perfect fingerprints.

<<Tatiana Kuzmowycz, 15>>

love is a poverty you couldn't sell / misery waiting in vague hotels / to be evicted —Beck, from "tropicalia"

WRITING TIP

Record your dreams. Keep a notebook and pen by your bed. The minute you wake up, write down every detail. Make dreams into poems, and poems into dreams.

She Bites Her Tongue

She bites her tongue
And stands up straight
Rolls her eyes
And fancies fate
Savors the thought
That it was all meant to
Plummet down creek
Reality smacks her in the face
And she brushes the blush onto her cheek
And maybe if she puts it on a little thick
The people will never know
She's anemic
And this is where the concealer goes
Underneath her eyes
She can't stop worrying herself awake
With yesterday's good-byes
Cherry lipstick
Feels so smooth
And then she rubs it in
If she colors them well
Perhaps no one will know where these
lips have been
Eyes are the window
To the soul
Well I suppose these eyes need shades
Look as feminine as you can
Until the mascara fades
She sees the swelling and is vividly
reminded
Of how much his words had stung
She closes her eyes
And bites her tongue

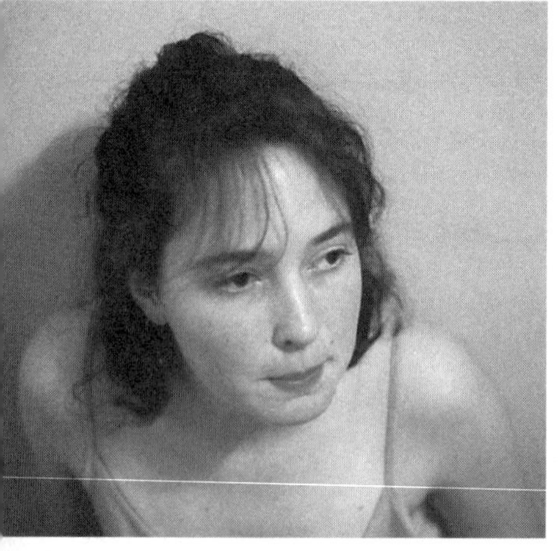

<<Elizabeth Seward, 15>>

YOU COME BACK

You come back into the room
Where you've been living
all along. You say:
What's been going on
while I was away? Who
got those sheets dirty, and why
are there no more grapefruit?
Setting foot on the middle ground
between body and word, which contains,
or is supposed to, other
people. You know it was you
who slept, who ate here, though you don't
believe it. I must have taken
time off, you think, for the buttered
toast and the love and maybe both
at once, which would account for the
grease on the bedspread, but no,
now you're certain, someone else
has been here wearing
your clothes and saying
words for you, because there was no time off.

—MARGARET ATWOOD

The better work men do is always done under stress and at great personal cost. —William Carlos Williams

WHAT'S YOUR

The days I can't put my finger on love are the days I write about it. Words on the page are the geography of head trying to make sense of the geography of heart. I rate the success of a poem by how much closer I have become acquainted with myself. If I have gained a greater understanding of my emotions that surround an experience, I have documented an important moment that I can never duplicate; a peach cannot taste the same way twice, a lover's kiss is familiar but never quite the same as the last one. I write about love so I never forget that it appears to me every day in different forms. The inky observations I share with paper help me recognize love and understand that when we think love's left for good, it hasn't—it has just decided to change shape.

—Dot Antoniades

Sometimes I can't remember when and where I've performed my poems because when I'm really conveying what they mean to me, I'm in my head back where they were written, the moment they hit me. "Wildish" is part of Atlanta at the end of R.E.M.'s Monster tour when she slipped her arm around my shoulder while he was on stage and said that we may never see this again, another moment of warm in a strange place.

—Douglas A. Martin

I write poems mostly about some form of injustice. Personal or political. Usually I dwell at length on some perceived slight or situation that appears to suck. And then I don't write about the situation, I write about the people.

—Jerry Quickley

INSPIRATION?

Q: What makes a slam superstar?

A: Anyone who writes it and says it like they mean it will do well at a slam. The best slam poets are wonderful entertainers. They're funny, they make you cry, and they're not afraid to be outrageous. And most of all, they are their poems. A talent like that deserves to become a household name, to be interviewed on TV, or star in a film. It could happen to you, if you write hard enough.

Q: Do slam poets tour?

A: The most active poets on the slam circuit try to make it to the bigger slams in major cities like New York, Chicago, San Francisco, and L.A. It's always fun to try your voice in a new town.

The real gold has always been the individual spirit...

—Tori Amos

THE WILD ONES

Pocahontas Grants an Interview With *Rolling Stone*

How did you hear about the role?
Disney wanted to resurrect an American Legend, as far as my agent told me, a real historical female heroine, none of that hackney Brother Grimm crap. Betsy Ross was their first choice but the editors had a hard time making a musical out of stars and shit. They wanted Helen Keller but they forgot she couldn't sing or dance.

Did you know that you'd get the role?
Sacajawea was considered but it would've taken the staff too long to research her trail. Being on a tight budget, it was easier for them to stay in Jamestown and take notes for a month.

What did you have to do to get the role?
I forgot my image would be on moccasins, coffee mugs and dolls. As soon as I did my screen test and Wardrobe had me try on my costume, execs said I had to lose weight and hired a physical trainer to give me a "Baywatch" figure. A stylist designed me a weave, super jet black extensions to add a dramatic effect when I ran through the hidden pine trails of the forests. Those extensions are now patented and you could purchase extensions for all sizes and colors at Bloomingdales. Each extension is carefully hand-woven by my tribe and contains .5% of my own hair and a portion of the profits will go for Pocaloca Land, a camping resort where kids can pick berries and meet white people settlers.

How strenuous was the role?
It was really awkward, running barefoot in a hoochie skirt. I wore skins my whole life but I'd gotten so used to wearing denims and a cotton T. Shooting on

location was cold, it took 16 hours to do "The Colors of the Wind" shoot and I mean I had to belt my tits off.

What was Mel Gibson like—playing John Smith?
I was nervous working with Mel and it was difficult reliving that part of my life. I have to admit, I was an out-of-control teen but I never got into John Smith.

Are there any eligible Hollywood men in your future?
The loves of my life are John Rolfe and my son. Honestly, the only reason I took the part was because I thought they'd tell my story: A Powhatan princess dying of smallpox in a Coney Island circus. They wanted a singing Wonder Woman who'd dodge speeding tomahawks to save a man bland as succotash. I'm not bionic. When you boil it all down, I'm just a maiden kayaking through life with the humming birds and otters.

What are your upcoming projects?
I'm opening the ribbon-cutting ceremony for the Pocahontas log cabin ride at EuroDisney and I've been offered the part in the musical theater version of "Dances With Wolves" on Broadway and George C. Wolfe wants me to do "Bring in Da T-Pee, Bring in Da Funk."

—Regie Cabico
(first performed at Urban Slam,
Gene Frankel Theater Basement,
New York City, 1998)

FAINTHEART IN A RAILWAY TRAIN

At nine in the morning there passed a church,

At ten there passed me by the sea,

At twelve a town of smoke and smirch,

At two a forest of oak and birch,

And then, on a platform, she:

A radiant stranger, who saw not me,

I said, "Get out to her do I dare?"

But I kept my seat in search for a plea,

And the wheels moved on. O could it but be

That I had alighted there!

—THOMAS HARDY

It Takes A Lot to Laugh It Takes A Train To Cry

Well, I ride on a mailtrain, babe
Can't buy a thrill
Well, I've been up all night
Leanin' on the window sill
Well, if I die
On top of the hill
And if I don't make it
You know my baby will.

Don't the moon look good, mama
Shinin' through the trees?
Don't the brakeman look good, mama
Ragging down the "Double E"?
Don't the sun look good
Goin' down over the sea?
Don't my gal look fine
When she's comin' after me?

Now the wintertime is coming
The windows are filled with frost
I went to tell everybody
But I could not get across
Well, I wanna be your lover, baby
I don't wanna be your boss
Don't say I never warned you
When your train gets lost.

—Bob Dylan

The secret to creativity is knowing how to hide your sources. —Albert Einstein

HALF LIGHT

atrocity number one,
simple son,
waltz into the room
in a green t-shirt
I smile with silver and a stick
of Winterfresh
and pull out my list
of what it's gonna take—
one more step
to fate
when am I gonna get to party—
live like I'm
not dying inside?
make me alive on train
seventy-five
got a powder
and a whole lot of pills
and a sonnet I wrote
just for you
sitting in the bottle of
my prime
watching silent vampire movies and
staring into the half light
wearing your old green
t-shirt
that looked too big on you,
anyway,
electro-magnetism
engineered for my safety
on track seventy-five
sent me home
in my own t-shirt
simplicity gave me nothing
but teenage tears
and a new pack of gum—
all poured into the bottle
of my prime

<<ASHLEY DAVIS, 16>>

Sometimes I feel you're sitting next to me and listening to my stories —Cibo Matto, from "Moonchild"

the quiet world

In an effort to get people to look
into each other's eyes more,
the government has decided to allot
each person exactly one hundred
and sixty-seven words, per day.

When the phone rings, I put it
to my ear without saying hello.
In the restaurant I point
at chicken noodle soup. I am
adjusting well to the new way.

Late at night, I call my long-
distance lover and proudly say:
I only used fifty-nine today.
I saved the rest for you.

When she doesn't respond, I know
she's used up all her words,
so I slowly whisper I love you,
thirty-two and a third times.
After that, we just sit on the line
and listen to each other breathe.

—Jeffrey McDaniel
(never performed)

Smoke-Filled Innocence

Cigarette smoke
filling her room
with pink bunnies and ballerinas
drinking like there's no end
til the world spins
and everything is just the same
dancing in the rain
wearing her little black dress
and high heels
seeing the world spin
and the stars glimmering
across the black velvet sky
shunning me because I'm not like
  you all
There's no drink in my hand
I'm not playing with a red straw
and laughing
I guess I don't belong
Our future is you
Cigarette smoke
pink ballerinas
and spinning stars

<<Tatiana Kuzmowycz, 15>>

WRITING TIP:

Everything around you is a potential poem. The ceiling, your breakfast cereal, boredom, your mom yelling at you to hurry up, love, your house when everyone is sleeping, the newspaper, summer, old sneakers, French kisses, half a glass of orange juice, the hairs in your hairbrush, and every molecule that breathes. No one owns this material, so use it. Art is free!

We Real Cool

The Pool Players.
Seven at the Golden Shovel.

We real cool. We
Left school. We

Lurk late. We
Strike straight. We

Sing sin. We
Thin gin. We

Jazz June. We
Die soon.

—Gwendolyn Brooks

Immature artists imitate. Mature artists steal. —Lionel Trilling

A Supermarket in California

What thoughts I have of you tonight, Walt Whitman, for I walked down the sidestreets under the trees with a headache self-conscious looking at the full moon.

In my hungry fatigue, and shopping for images, I went into the neon fruit supermarket, dreaming of your enumerations!

What peaches and what penumbras! Whole families shopping at night! Aisles full of husbands! Wives in the avocados, babies in the tomatoes!—and you, Garciá Lorca, what were you doing down by the watermelons?

I saw you, Walt Whitman, childless, lonely old grubber, poking among the meats in the refrigerator and eyeing the grocery boys.

I heard you asking questions of each: Who killed the pork chops? What price bananas? Are you my Angel?

I wandered in and out of the brilliant stacks of cans following you, and followed in my imagination by the store detective.

We strode down the open corridors together in our solitary fancy tasting artichokes, possessing every frozen delicacy, and never passing the cashier.

Where are we going, Walt Whitman? The doors close in an hour. Which way does your beard point tonight?

(I touch your book and dream of our odyssey in the supermarket and feel absurd.)

Will we walk all night through solitary streets? The trees add shade to shade, lights out in the houses, we'll both be lonely.

Will we stroll dreaming of the lost America of love past blue automobiles in driveways, home to our silent cottage?

Ah, dear father, graybeard, lonely old courage-teacher, what America did you have when Charon quit poling his ferry and you got out on a smoking bank and stood watching the boat disappear on the black waters of Lethe?

—Allen Ginsberg

howl

allen ginsberg
told me
that I was beautiful
in a new york city café
and I thought
he was trying to
pick me up.

you can imagine how arrogant chinese boys in new
    york get about love when old
gay white men are involved.

exactly eleven months later,
he died.

the distance between point A and B
can be measured in days,
but friendship hates math
and so the sum of experiences
between two people
is not a sum,
it's
eating blintzes under trees,
learning how cézanne liked to color
and
sitting in bed,
debating the value of failure in one's life,
and seeing allen
read one last time in front of 680 NYU kids
that had no idea
he would spend
the next week in boston
starting his negotiations
with death.

my friend is dead
and I don't know
how to approach the subject.

my generation has no starving, hysterical nakeds.
I'm a member of the fame whore, superstar-at-any-cost-we-
could-give-a-fuck-
about-a-fuck-because-teen-angst-isn't-enough-anymore-our-
self-absorbed-
natures-have-overkilled-into-egomaniacal-dynamo-rage club

and
we don't know
the first thing about
the words
"selfless"
or
"give."

I mean,
fuck the fact that he's gay,
a beatnik,
and that even I get bored
with his poetry,
the ginz made tibet a cause to believe in,
he pushed the angry buttons of politicians for four decades,
and
he set fire to one hundred and thirty-seven million minds
in this world,
becoming lou reed, bob dylan, billy burroughs, and my answer
to the question
"who has influenced you in this life?"

sure,
some days he came off
as an asshole,
but most of us aren't in the public eye enough
to be caught
in our asshole moments.

but for each of those asshole moments
there is the simple beauty

of him cooking mushroom omelettes,
and
him exposing me to buddhism (a culture my
ancestors taught him),
and his wiley, old man eyes
correcting me and saying,
"you have a long way to go if you want to be a good writer."

don't try and dull my memories of him
at point A
I ran with his mind in a 13th St. loft
because his legs
were no longer capable
of adventures on foot,
to point B
when I sat silent by the phone,
listening to him say
four days before his death
that he thought
he had another month.

point B to point C
is a distance I'm not sure I'll ever reach,
as I try and find straight lines,
reading his work in Barnes & Noble,
and
remembering how he talked
about his first connections to kerouac
with a certain reverie,
and
I don't know if I'll ever realize the scope of the words "death"
or "good-bye,"
but I'm getting that little ache under the ribcage
from loss
and the need to finally
tell a friend,
"I love you."

—Beau Sia

Beau Sia

Poets are jails. Works are the convicts who escape.—Jean Cocteau

for the mad

you will be alone at last
in the sanity of your friends.

brilliance will fade away from you
and you will settle in dimmed light.

you will not remember how to mourn
your dying difference.

you will not be better but
they will say you are well.

—Lucille Clifton

WRITING TIP

Write a poem about exactly what you were doing and thinking and smelling and hearing, etc. the moment you heard some major news, good or bad. Dig deep. Find connections.

Paperdoll People

Your plastic eyes search my figure
So different from yours
Unique and hideous
A creature you have never seen

You shake me violently, and turn me over
Looking for my seam
The place of imperfection
Where you can rip me apart and find out
what I am made of

I am different from you
And it scares you
I have disrupted your neat order
Your common sense geometric world

You hate me
And all because I chose to be my own person
But I am not you
And I am not like you

Though I want to be like you
I try to stand in your rows of paperdoll people
And I pretend that you won't notice
But I am always found out

I want to be accepted
But I refuse to be like you
The happy medium I'm searching for
is nowhere to be found

So I sit by myself, cowering
Hiding in the corner of our world
Watching as the single file lines
Of paperdoll people go by.

<< Stefanie Wilde, 15>>

Stuff to Do In Saratoga When You're Bored

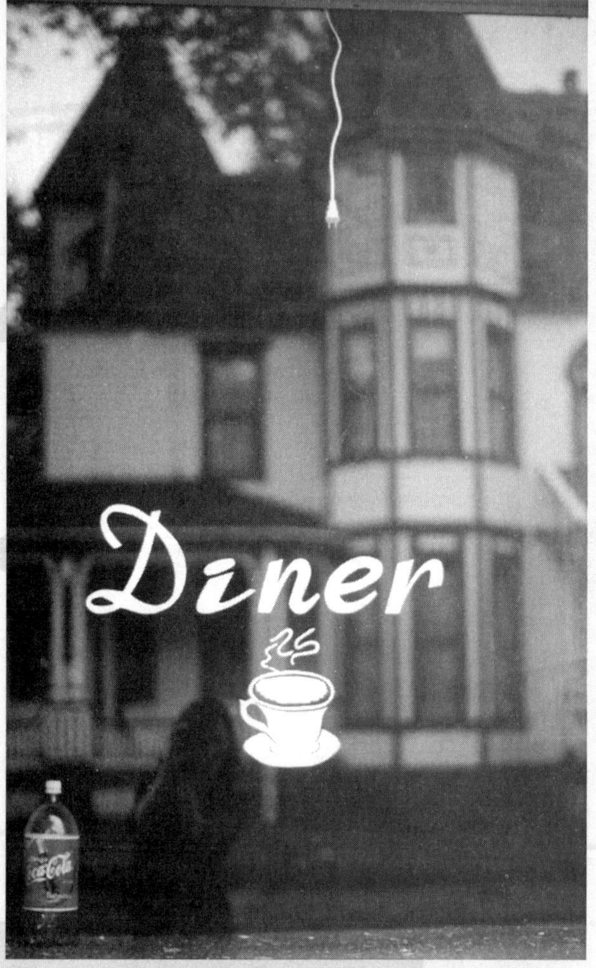

It was tough to grow up in the suburbs. For every pot-smoking hesher or combustible jock, there was a normal kid who didn't want to hang out at the mall or go to the pep rally. We had to think of other options. Like forming the Church of Chuck Woolery. My friend's sister painted a beautiful portrait of Chuck surrounded by an angelic golden glow. We'd exchange little tidbits about Chuck's life, or wonder aloud, "What would Chuck do in a situation like this?"

At the commercial break on *Love Connection* when Chuck said he'd be back in "two minutes and two seconds"—he often just flashed a grin and a peace sign and said, "Two and two"—we'd get out our watches and time it, cheering him on. Chuck was always right as rain. This entertained us for about a month. Why worship Satan when there are so many game show hosts worthy of their very own cult?

Another fun diversion was to make up fake stories and call the local newspaper. My friend Nicole held the title for this one. Without letting anyone else in on the prank, she convinced a local reporter that she rose each morning at 3 a.m. to sweep the streets of the town. She said she wanted to give something back to the community that had done so much for her.

They came to her house while her parents were at work, photographed her out in the street with a push broom and ran a full page story with a 'local teens aren't all bad' type of angle. The congratulatory letters came pouring in from her former teachers and various senior citizens. And of course, the kids at school decided she was even weirder than they thought.

The local 7-11 was the place to find out where the parties were. Sometimes you didn't even have to pull into the parking lot. You could just hear some thick-necked jock bellowing "Off Sobey Road, dude!" out of his Bronco over to the big-hair girls in the Mazda RX-7. We'd follow behind, in our humble wood-paneled stationwagon, park far away from the house, and then commando around the yard until we found an open door or window. We'd sneak inside, find a room that no one was in, hide out, and eavesdrop. There is nothing like the scintillating conversation of girls with mohair sweaters and sticky lipgloss drinking wine coolers. Or guys in too-tight jeans, big L. L. Bean sweaters, desert boots, and denim jackets with sheepskin collars pounding Bud after Bud bragging about who they are having sex with while their parents are out of town.

We played board games on the roof of the bank downtown. This was also a good spot to watch our favorite student couples get in fights as they left local restaurants. We wore wigs and frumpy sweatsuits, and drank four or five pots of coffee at Denny's. This once led us to flesh out a crude musical about Denny's. All the songs were composed on napkins and sugar packets. We had vignettes about greasy ladyfingers, Grand Slam breakfasts, and our favorite employees like Joseph, the ex-military computer student, and Bib, the grandmother of nine.

We scaled the foothills and snuck in to see the shows during the Paul Masson Winery Summer Concert Series. We never got caught. Who would ever suspect teenagers of breaking the law to scope out Sergio Mendez or Smokey Robinson? By purchasing one $30 ticket and hiding people in the trunk, drive-in movie style, we also got to see James Brown, Ray Charles and Ella Fitzgerald.

We didn't boycott the prom because it was stupid. You had to check it out at least once. We brought a large watermelon and danced only with it during the slow songs. For the fast songs, we dragged one of the parent chaperones out on the floor and went crazy. We didn't just play air guitar. We played air keyboards and air saxophone. Attached toilet paper to our shoes and pretended not to understand why everyone was making fun of us. Asked Mr. Suave if he wanted a cigar and then put a Tampax in his breast pocket. Stepped back and enjoyed his reaction as he was disgusted at the thought of retrieving a paper-wrapped piece of cotton. (For the older set, this also works in retro nightclubs!)

We would go to Safeway and rearrange the displays. The best one was the Healthy Heart display. Item by item, we replaced the oat bran muffins, apples, and black beans until underneath the huge sign that read 'Make Your Heart Healthy and Happy' was an exhibit of cigarettes, bourbon, bologna, and Ding Dongs.

This is just a small sampling of ways we dealt with teenage suburban existence. And if I can help even one kid survive until graduation, I'll feel that I have made a difference. Go Falcons!

—Beth Lisick

Poetry and Hums aren't things which you get, they're things which get you. And all you can do is go where they can find you. —A.A. Milne, as said by Winnie-the-Pooh

haikus

Hailing yellow cabs,
But choose subway fares instead.
Cold plastic not plush.

Currents of people,
Rushing down Park Avenue.
Salaries to earn.

A fluorescent night.
The city that never sleeps.
Silence is golden.

<<Alicia Lopez, 18>>

On My Own

As the hum of the radio fades in and
out, I look at the everlasting
road.
The yellow line seems to go on forever
and the road can be seen far in
the
distance.
The tires make a grinding noise as it
rolls along the road, that has
long needed to be
paved.
And as I stare out the dirt-stained window, we pass places I don't know.
Yet, they still seem familiar, and their
presence comforts me.
I lay my head back on the torn seats,
hoping to be able to sleep.
The seats smell of smoke, reminding
me of my father's cigars.
Suddenly the car comes to a halt, and
we've reached my destination.
I step out of the rusted taxi, and the
fresh air greets me with a gentle
gust
of wind.
I pay the driver, and as I walk up the
stairs towards my dorm,
I feel a chill go down my spine.
This is it, I am on my own.

<<Natalie Maher, 14>>

I'M NOBODY, WHO ARE YOU?

I'm nobody. Who are you?
Are you nobody too?
Then there's a pair of us.
Don't tell—they'd banish us, you know.

How dreary to be somebody,
How public—like a frog—
To tell your name the livelong June
To an admiring bog.

—EMILY DICKINSON

Watching E.T. After a Day of Kosovo and Diallo on the Nightly News

I haven't seen E.T.
since I was four years old, but tonight I grab the night-
blue videotape
from among my collection of X-Files episodes and
home videos.
When E.T. dies, when Elliot's brother Michael swears,
I am shocked as I never was
nine years ago, when my father brought home
"the story
that touched the world"
for the first time. Then,
I must have known that E.T.'s spaceship would come
back for him,
as my preschool class always found me
when I was lost on field trips;
I must have believed that the power of Elliot's
love could bring E.T.
back to life. Tonight, I cry just like everyone else
when the boy and the lost alien point to their hearts
and say,
"Ouch." I couldn't have known, when I was four,
that I could be hurt this badly by a movie,
while during the day we drop bombs on other countries
and convict police officers
of murder. Tonight I think Elliot is the lucky one;
at ten, he can hold tight to E.T. forever and never
let go. At midnight I turn out the light and go to bed,
saline still clinging to my lashes; they will be crusty
with salt
tomorrow morning, but I don't want to think anymore
tonight.

<<Rachel Nobel, 16>>

Life can only be what you make it / When you're feelin down / You should never fake it —Mary J. Blige, from "My Life"

The Day Lady Died

It is 12 : 20 in New York a Friday
three days after Bastille day, yes
it is 1959 and I go get a shoeshine
because I will get off the 4 : 19 in Easthampton
at 7 : 15 and then go straight to dinner
and I don't know the people who will feed me

I walk up the muggy street beginning to sun
and have a hamburger and a malted and buy
an ugly NEW WORLD WRITING to see what the poets
in Ghana are doing these days
                                        I go on to the bank
and Miss Stillwagon (first name Linda I once heard)
doesn't even look up my balance for once in her life
and in the GOLDEN GRIFFIN I get a little Verlaine
for Patsy with drawings by Bonnard although I do
think of Hesiod, trans. Richmond Lattimore or
Brendan Behan's new play or *Le Balcon* or *Les Nègres*
of Genet, but I don't, I stick with Verlaine
after practically going to sleep with quandariness

and for Mike I just stroll into the PARK LANE
Liquor Store and ask for a bottle of Strega and
then I go back to where I came from to 6th Avenue
and the tobacconist in the Ziegfeld Theatre and
casually ask for a carton of Gauloises and a carton
of Picayunes, and a NEW YORK POST with her face on it

and I am sweating a lot by now and thinking of
leaning on the john door in the 5 SPOT
while she whispered a song along the keyboard
to Mal Waldron and everyone and I stopped breathing

—Frank O'Hara

SONGWRITERS

Basically I think it is one of the greatest things is when someone is expressive and shows a bit of their vulnerability and honesty in whatever they do, whether you're a plumber or a doctor, a painter, a dancer, a writer, or a trash collector—I mean everyone's got a creative side. It's really just up to them to search and find it.

—Beth Hart

Songwriting to me means individuality. I think society sometimes makes us feel like we should follow set rules, and for some people that may be good, but for others it's definitely not. Writing helps go against the norm of society and makes you an individual, and individuals are what make up a society. Songwriting helps bring that out. It's a therapy for me at times. Usually when I write it is not when I'm in the best frame of mind. I think everyone needs some kind of escape, some way to deal with their down time, and also the time to figure out who they are.

—Ed Roland, Collective Soul

Sometimes I have the music first and I listen to it and work from there. I can do it alone, or I can write with everybody around. I can do it on planes, whatever. It's just when it hits me, I do it. . . . I write about how I feel or how I feel about somebody else. It could be something about me, or it could be something about you that I can relate to. Sometimes I use writing as a way to deal with problems or to get through something happening in my life. Like when something is driving you crazy and you just want to get it off. Writing helps.

—Mary J. Blige

SOUND OFF

I find that most of the musical or literary works that I connect with started with a writer who was connected emotionally with what he or she was writing. I think that's why, as a writer, I try to write without an agenda, only letting out what comes out naturally.

In music, the business end of things can take the shine off your work. Soon they'll call it product, and it feels like it's out of your hands to a degree. That's why the most important part about writing is in the conception. When it's you and you alone.

—Rob Thomas, Matchbox Twenty

For me poetry allowed words to be given to the things that otherwise had no voice, and I discovered the strength and soul of poetry—through it we come to know; we are led to feel, sense, and to expand our understanding beyond words.

—Jewel

When you can let go of your feelings in songs, that gets everything off your chest. For me, to be able to put it on wax and let people see how I really feel on an every day basis makes me feel relaxed, more at ease than just being closed up, not saying anything. I think being able to express myself to the world, and let people know, "Hey, I go through problems, too," has pretty much helped me get through the day.

—Missy Elliott

Poetry is what in a poem makes you laugh, cry, prickle, be silent, makes your toenails twinkle, makes you want to do this or that or nothing, makes you know that you are alone in the unknown world, that your bliss and suffering is forever shared and forever all your own.

—Dylan Thomas

GETTING IT DOWN

they call her reality

she is the no girl.

a lost soul.

she comes out at night

when the rain falls. heavy.

she likes it that way.

no one speaks to her

except the wet grass . . .

and maybe the thundering

sky . . .

she is alone

<< Leah Blumer, 15>>

A poem is made up of thoughts, each of which filled the whole sky of the poet in its turn. –Ralph Waldo Emerson

MOON!
MOON!
I AM PRONE BEFORE YOU.
PITY ME,
AND DRENCH ME IN LONELINESS.

—AMY LOWELL

SELF-INVOLVEMENT AT ITS BEST

midnight comes too soon at
college.
i sit here at a dell optiplex—
emily spoke of a certain slant of light,
but i sit here
and consider how you ended a letter—
if you said something nice,
and if you did, how do i respond—
keats compared the song of a nightingale
to wine—
but i can't seem to get past
scattered emails,
can't get outside of room 204
in shaw hall
can't get outside of the tri county area—
too involved in away messages
to pray or listen to anyone else talk.
i miss my ninth grade bedroom,
my fifth grade best friend,
and the time i got high with robin.
the clock spins
and orange minutes dissolve like alka seltzer,
duritz said it doesn't get much worse than this—
it does.
it's not Tuesday—it's everyday
times a million.
twenty-seven lines of selfishness—
let's make it twenty-eight.

<<ELIZABETH ADAMS, 19>>

Either the Darkness Alters—

Or Something in the Sight

Adjusts itself to Midnight—

And Life steps almost straight.

— Emily Dickinson

In a forest pitch-dark / glowed the tiniest spark / it burst into flame / Like me —Bjork, from "Isobel"

I'll take a quiet life / a handshake some carbon monoxide / no alarms and no surprises
—Radiohead, from "no surprises"

The Red Wheelbarrow

So much depends
upon

a red wheel
barrow

glazed with rain
water

beside the white
chickens

—William Carlos Williams

WRITING TIP

Turn off the TV and go outside

WELL THEY SHOOED ME AWAY
FROM HERE THE TIME BEFORE
TURNED THEIR BACKS
AND THEY LOCKED THEIR DOORS
I'M WATCHIN' TV IN
THE WINDOW OF A FURNITURE STORE

—TOM WAITS, FROM "COLD WATER"

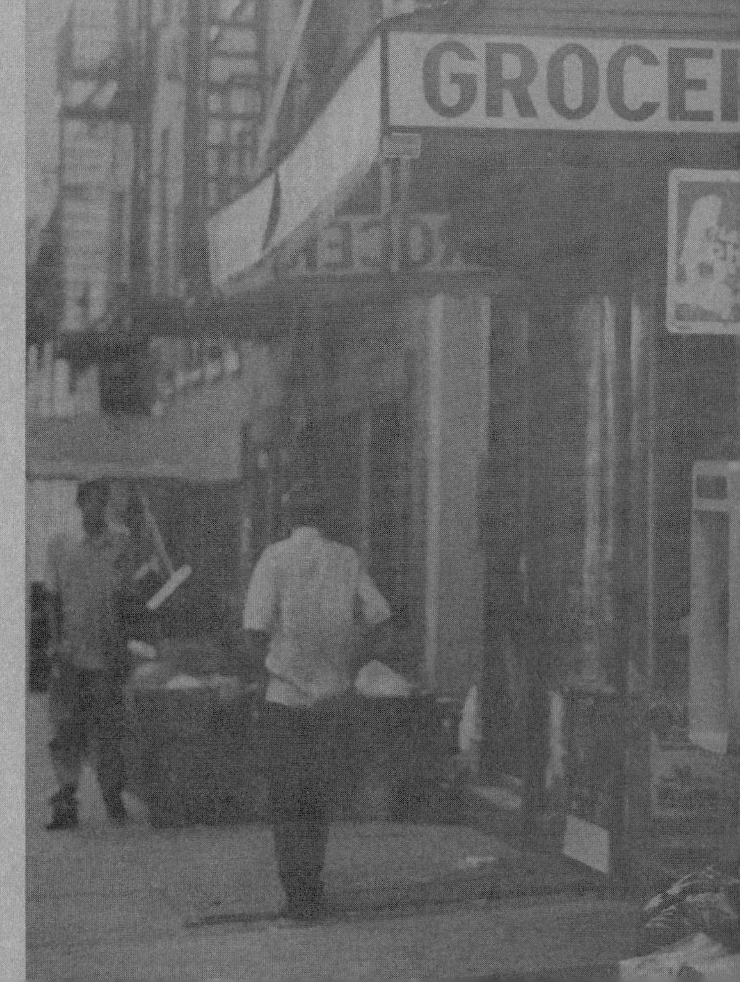

SONNET NUMBER 80

O how I faint when I of you do write,
Knowing a better spirit doth use your name,
And in the praise thereof spends all his might,
To make me tongue-tied, speaking of your fame.
But since your worth (wide as the ocean is)
The humble as the proudest sail doth bear,
My saucy bark (inferior far to his)
On your broad main doth willfully appear.
Your shallowest help will hold me up afloat,
Whilst he upon your soundless deep doth ride,
Or (being wrack'd) I am a worthless boat,
He of tall building and of goodly pride.

—WILLIAM SHAKESPEARE

Escape

Arm in arm
we fade against the horizon
in a backwards birth.
We never existed
a great relief.
Life was a hallucination
inspired by electrical spasms
pounding in the matter
of our brains.
Thankful to know
only each other
and to be known
only by one another.
Grateful
for the watercolor horizon
Comforted to be characters
invented by the mind
of a twisted writer
in a world
unbeknownst to us
in a book
unbeknownst to anyone.
We sail away
floating on intensity
and peace
smiling sleepily
beneath a gleaming moon
setting off for a world
of our own creation.
For a world of our own escape.

<< Iris Moulton, 14>>

Poetry is a river . . . —Mary Oliver

WRITING TIP

Writer's block? Go for a walk. Movement makes your mind work.

A WHITE WHISPER

In the distance
I hear
a white whisper
The poplar trees
sway
with the sultry wind
The beauty of it all
knows no bounds
nor does the whisper
Behind me
the pine trees
mimic their friends
The swaying
continues
refusing to cease
But gently
whispers
in the serenity

<< AUDREY LAFAVE, 15>>

To read a poem is to hear it with our eyes; to hear it is to see it with our ears. —Octavio Paz

I don't need much to keep me warm
Got a cloud sleeping on my tongue
he goes
then it goes
and kiss the violets as they're waking up

– Tori Amos, from "Cloud on My Tongue"

Why I Am Not a Painter

I am not a painter, I am a poet.
Why? I think I would rather be
a painter, but I am not. Well,

for instance, Mike Goldberg
is starting a painting. I drop in.
"Sit down and have a drink" he
says. I drink; we drink. I look
up. "You have SARDINES in it."
"Yes, it needed something there."
"Oh." I go and the days go by
and I drop in again. The painting
is going on, and I go, and the days
go by. I drop in. The painting is
finished. "Where's SARDINES?"
All that's left is just
letters. "It was too much," Mike says.

But me? One day I am thinking of
a color: orange. I write a line
about orange. Pretty soon it is a
whole page of words, not lines.

Then another page. There should be
so much more, not of orange, of
words, of how terrible orange is
and life. Days go by. It is even in
prose, I am a real poet. My poem
is finished and I haven't mentioned
orange yet. It's twelve poems, I call
it ORANGES. And one day in a gallery
I see Mike's painting, called SARDINES.

—Frank O'Hara

Ut pictura poesis.—As in painting, so in poetry. —Horace

BRUNSWICK®
Sardines
in SOYBEAN OIL
NET WT. 3.75 OZ (106g)
INGREDIENTS: SARDINES,
SOYBEAN OIL, SALT.
0 66613 00005 9

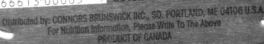

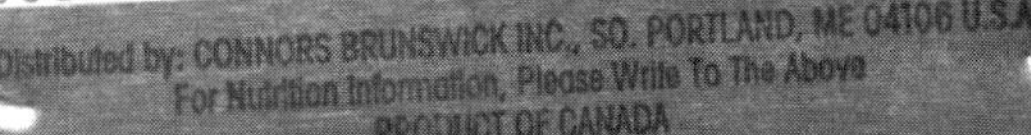
Distributed by: CONNORS BRUNSWICK INC., SO. PORTLAND, ME 04106 U.S.A.
For Nutrition Information, Please Write To The Above
PRODUCT OF CANADA

Without freedom, no art; art lives only on the restraints it imposes on itself, and dies of all others. —Albert Camus

As I watch from my window

a portal to thy world abroad

An unfamiliar shadow looms

I focus on this form

a rival shadow

That points towards a trail of risks

Risks that daunt

that fashion to build a world so distant

<<Uche Anyanwu, 15>>

When I Have Fears

When I have fears that I may cease to be
    Before my pen has gleaned my teeming brain,
Before high-piléd books, in charact'ry,
    Hold like rich garnets the full-ripened grain;
When I behold, upon the night's starred face,
    Huge cloudy symbols of a high romance,

And think that I may never live to trace
    Their shadows, with the magic hand of chance;
And when I feel, fair creature of an hour,
    That I shall never look upon thee more,
Never have relish in the faery power
    Of unreflecting love!—then on the shore
Of the wide world I stand alone, and think
Till Love and Fame to nothingness do sink.

— John Keats

WRITING TIP

Separate your senses. First, describe a random object as it meets your sense of smell. Write until your brain is about to explode. Then see it, taste it, touch and hear it in succession.

Make a poem from what you have written.

it's cold outside

we
are an inevitability
because i called it
like I call the front seat
on road trips
"I got shotgun"

you the
scenery
and destination
solved the riddle
in my smile
on the first try

didn't have to guess
had the answers to the test
or a copy of the
teacher's edition
handed down
by an older sibling
who took the same class
last year

lashes like daddy long legs
sweep doubt from my cheek
eyes squint to see

you more clearly

your lips to my ear
spoke words
women everywhere
been wanting waiting
to hear

(yeah)
we're an inevitability

like growing older
losing baby teeth

you will love me
with the same ease
that you recite the lyrics
of your favorite song

the potential of this
is the feeling fifth graders get
when snow falls
and starts to stick

you are the prospect

Art is a step from what is obvious and well-known toward what is arcane and concealed. —Kahlil Gibran

You may say I'm a dreamer / But I'm not the only one / I hope someday you'll join us... —John Lennon, "Imagine"

of a half-day of school
i am the free time
in the afternoon

eyes talk too much so
our reflections
avoid each other
as we let our knees touch

the collective will
of a math class
can make the snow fall faster

i called this
the snow will stick
we have the afternoon
to ourselves
what
do you want to do
with it?

—Felice Belle
(first performed in a friend's apartment
in New York City)

felice belle

its all me

its not my fault that my dark hair transforms
from black to pink to yellow like a backwards sunset
or a forward sunrise

and its not my fault i like to sit in my room and jam on the bass
pretending that i have lots of talent like im actually in a productive band
like we actually have records and fans that arent our best friends

and its not bad that i go to shows
and skank and mosh and yell out all the words
even the ones my mother wouldnt approve of,
the ones she'd take soap to my mouth for until i coughed up bubbles
and she got worried and stopped and i said thanks

theres nothing wrong with having ambition that's not apparent to anyone
but me
like my secret ambition to be a rock star in the CIA
kicking in doors by day but
screaming and strumming in smoky clubs for the kids i used to be

theres nothing wrong with surfing every day that i breathe
from the time i wake up till the time i look like a raisin
and im cold and shivering and completely happy because today the waves were
totally wicked and so was i
there's nothing wrong with that and there's nothing wrong with me

<<Lauren Orso, 14>>

HERE IN THIS MOMENT TO MYSELF

I'M GONNA VIBE WITH NO ONE ELSE

THERE IS A CONVERSATION I NEED TO HAVE WITH ME

IT'S JUST A MOMENT TO MYSELF

— MACY GRAY, FROM "A MOMENT TO MYSELF"

A poet is a nightingale, who sits in darkness and sings to cheer its own solitude with sweet sounds.
—Percy Bysshe Shelley

Phenomenal Woman

Pretty women wonder where my
  secret lies.
I'm not cute or built to suit a fashion
  model's size
But when I start to tell them,
They think I'm telling lies.
I say,
It's in the reach of my arms
The span of my hips,
The stride of my step,
The curl of my lips.
I'm a woman
Phenomenally.
Phenomenal woman,
That's me.

I walk into a room
Just as cool as you please,
And to a man,
The fellows stand or
Fall down on their knees.
Then they swarm around me,
A hive of honey bees.
I say,
It's the fire in my eyes,
And the flash of my teeth,
The swing in my waist,
And the joy in my feet.
I'm a woman
Phenomenally.
Phenomenal woman,
That's me.

Men themselves have wondered
What they see in me.
They try so much
But they can't touch
My inner mystery.
When I try to show them
They say they still can't see.
I say,
It's the arch of my back,
The sun of my smile,
The ride of my breasts,
The grace of my style.
I'm a woman
Phenomenally.
Phenomenal woman,
That's me.

Now you understand
Just why my head's not bowed.
I don't shout or jump about
Or have to talk real loud.
When you see me passing
It ought to make you proud.
I say,
It's in the click of my heels,
The bend of my hair,
The palm of my hand,
The need of my care.
'Cause I'm a woman
Phenomenally.
Phenomenal woman,
That's me.

— Maya Angelou

I too am not a bit tamed . . . . too am untranslatable,/I sound my barbaric yawp over the roofs of the world.
—Walt Whitman, from *Song of Myself*

FROM THE PAGE

On the creative process:

I could tell you my creative process, but then I'd have to kill you. Let me just say that first and foremost on my "keep this in mind when you're writing" list is being myself. From there, any number of unlistable things lend to my creative process. And the inspiration for that process? The muse that drives it all? Love, death, women.

– Beau Sia

On the muse:

Inspiration is everywhere. But you have to actively seek it. There are poems waiting for you on the #4 train, on the evening news, or a in a conversation overheard on the street. If I sat at my computer waiting for inspiration to hit me, I might never write another poem. So I go out with my pen and my notebook and absorb as much as I can.

– Felice Belle

On writing:

The page is always the safest material to talk to–whether it holds the inky outpour of raw emotion or several years' worth of editing. I always try to let my journal be the place where I write without thinking I'm going to be judged. From there I decide whether or not I want to sculpt a piece for an audience to absorb aurally. The page and the stage are two different animals.

–Dot Antoniades

TO THE STAGE

Why slam?

It's a really powerful thing to see a complete stranger on the stage, telling a private and hidden part of your story. Slam poets are the tribe's historians. They record the way we are kind and cruel to each other.

—Jerry Quickley

Advice for the young poet:

Read Read Read if you want to be a poet   take a class   go to a museum   study quilt making   listen to what's out there   keep writing and then learn to shed your words   until you can't shed anymore   have courage and find the joy in your life   hold it and never stray away from what scares you

—Regie Cabico

Q: Where can I find a slam near me?

A: Check out listings in your local paper or weekly area magazine. Most slams happen at night, so they'll probably be listed in the "Night Life" section. Read the bulletin boards at your local bookstore, your favorite café, the local college library. Ask around. The poetry slam is a rapidly growing phenomenon, so there are most likely slams happening within a short traveling distance.

bios and credits

Tori Amos began singing and playing piano in her church choir. At the age of thirteen she gave up a scholarship to study the piano at Baltimore's Peabody Conservatory so she could perform her own material in Washington, D.C. clubs. With the release of her 1992 debut album, *Little Earthquakes*, Amos built an intense and loyal following that continues to grow to this day.

Maya Angelou, an American writer whose work explores the themes of racial, economic, and sexual oppression. *I Know Why the Caged Bird Sings* is her best-known book. Among her many honors, she composed and delivered a poem for the inauguration of President Bill Clinton in 1993.

Dot Antoniades contributed work to *Skyscrapers, Taxis & Tampons*, a women's poetry anthology. She has performed her own work at various New City venues, including the Nuyorican Poets Café, which she represented in the 1997 National Slam Tournament. She is the former host of the Nuyorican Poets Café Slam Open and has a B.F.A. in acting from Marymount Manhattan College.

Matthew Arnold (1822–88), English Victorian poet and literary and social critic, was well known for his attacks on the contemporary tastes and manners of the times.

Margaret Atwood has had eleven volumes of poetry published in Canada, the United States, and sixteen other countries. She is also a successful novelist.

W. H. Auden (1907–73), English-born poet and man of letters, believed in the notion of poetry as a form of therapy similar to psychoanalysis.

Cheryl B. is a writer and seven-year veteran of the spoken-word scene in her native New York. She has performed her work in London, Paris, Sydney, and the Pacific Northwest. Her poetry has appeared in various literary journals, 'zines, and anthologies, including *Poetry Nation*, *The World in Us*, and *Revival: Spoken Word from Lollapalooza*.

Erykah Badu is one of the fastest-rising American recording artists. Just one year after the release of her phenomenally successful 1997 debut album, *Baduizm*, Badu played a supporting role in the film *The Cider House Rules*.

Honoré de Balzac (1799–1850) was a French writer who was considered to be an extraordinary observer and chronicler of French society.

Beastie Boys, consisting of New Yorkers Adam "MCA" Yauch, Adam "Ad-Rock" Horovitz, and Mike "Mike D" Diamond, have released seven highly creative albums that merge elements of hip-hop, punk, funk, and hard core with a political twist.

Beck (Hansen) draws on pseudopoetry, hip-hop, folk, experimental rock, psychedelia, and pop to create a junk-culture brand of postmodern music.

Felice Belle is a graduate student at New York University's Gallatin School of Individualized Study and teaches poetry part-time to fifth graders at PS 165 in Flushing, Queens. Belle is the host of the Friday Night Slam at the Nuyorican Poets Café in New York City.

Bjork quickly eclipsed the popularity of her old band, avant-pop group The Sugarcubes, with her dynamic solo career. Hailing from Reykjavik, Iceland, Bjork has been a professional vocalist since she was a child.
William Blake (1757–1827), English poet, painter, and engraver, is regarded as one of the greatest figures of romanticism. Blake was ignored by the public of his day and lived and died in poverty.
Mary J. Blige was dubbed the "Queen of Hip-Hop Soul" at the age of twenty-one. She was raised in Yonkers, New York, and performed in local groups before recording her debut album, *What's the 411?*
Georges Braque (1882–1963), French painter, was a revolutionary of twentieth-century art who, together with Pablo Picasso, developed cubism.
Gwendolyn Brooks is an American poet whose works deal with the everyday life of urban blacks. She was the first African-American poet to win the Pulitzer Prize (1949), and in 1968 she was named poet laureate of Illinois.
Dana Bryant is a former Grand Slam Champion of the Nuyorican Poets Café. She is a Warner Brothers recording artist/poet—one of the first slam poets to cross over to that medium.
Regie Cabico is the winner of the 1993 Nuyorican Poets Café Slam. He participated in the 1993, 1994, and 1997 National Poetry Slams and took first place in 1997 with *Mouth Almighty, Manhattan*. He is co-editor of *Poetry Nation: The North American Anthology of Fusion Poetry*.
Ray Charles is perhaps the musician most responsible for the development of soul music. He remains one of the most emotional and easily identifiable performers of the twentieth century.
Anton Chekhov (1860–1904), Russian playwright and master of the modern short story, is regarded as the outstanding representative of the late-nineteenth-century Russian realist school. *Ivanov*, *Uncle Vanya*, and *The Cherry Orchard* are three of his finest dramatic works.
Cibo Matto, Italian for "food madness," is a Japanese-born duo who relocated to New York City where their pop melodies created a sensation amongst the Lower Manhattan hipster elite. Their second album, *Stereo Type A*, topped the indie charts in 1999.
Lucille Clifton is an American poet who employs black vernacular in her examinations of family relationships and life in the urban ghetto. Clifton's work reflects her pride in being an African-American woman and a poet.
Jean Cocteau (1889–1963), French poet, novelist, actor, and film director, was best known for his poem *L'Ange Heurtebise* (*The Angel Heurtebise*).
Paula Cole, winner of 1998's Grammy for best new artist, is one of the many female singer-songwriters who rose to prominence in the 1990s. Her single "I Don't Want to Wait" is the theme song for the hit TV show *Dawson's Creek*.
Samuel Taylor Coleridge (1772–1834) was an English lyrical poet, critic, and philosopher. His lyrical ballads, written with William Wordsworth, heralded the English romantic movement.
E. E. Cummings (1894–1962), American poet and painter, first attracted attention for his eccentric phrasing and punctuation. Cummings's name is often styled "e. e. cummings" in the mistaken

belief that the poet legally changed his name to lowercase letters only.

Emily Dickinson (1830–86), American lyric poet, referred to as "the New England Mystic," experimented with poetic rhythms and rhymes. Although extremely prolific, the majority of her poetry was published posthumously.

Ani DiFranco is one of the most inspirational and influential cult heroines of the 1990s. DiFranco releases her records on her own independent label, Righteous Babe, and has steadily built a devoted following on the strength of a never-ending tour schedule.

Fyodor Dostoyevsky (1821–81), Russian novelist and short story writer, is regarded as one of the finest novelists who ever lived. Dostoyevsky's works were often called prophetic because he so accurately predicted how Russia's revolutionaries would behave if they came into power.

Bob Dylan, American musician, infused his rock and roll lyrics with the intellectualism of classic literature and poetry. He is considered the greatest songwriter and iconic spokesman of his generation.

Albert Einstein (1879–1955) was a German-American physicist recognized as one of the most creative intellects in human history. His theories of relativity and gravitation revolutionized scientific and philosophical inquiry. Einstein won the Nobel Prize in physics in 1921.

T. S. Eliot (1888-1965), American poet, playwright, literary critic, and editor, was the leader of the Modernist movement. His experimentation with diction, style, and verse revitalized English poetry. Eliot's best-known works include *The Waste Land* and *The Love Song of J. Alfred Prufrock.*

Missy "Misdemeanor" Elliott has emerged as one of the most innovative hip-hop record producers and performers of the 1990s.

Ralph Waldo Emerson (1803–82), American poet, essayist and lecturer, was a defining figure of New England transcendentalism. He spent two years living in solitude at the edge of a pond. This experience produced *Walden*, one of his best known works.

F. Scott Fitzgerald (1846–1940), best known for his novels and short stories, chronicled the excesses of America's Jazz Age during the 1920s. He is as famous for his extravagant lifestyle as he is for his novels, *The Great Gatsby*, *Tender Is the Night*, and *The Beautiful and the Damned.*

Anna Freud (1895–1982), the youngest daughter of Dr. Sigmund Freud, was the British founder of child psychoanalysis and one of its foremost practitioners.

Robert Frost (1874–1963), American poet, was much admired for his depictions of New England rural life and his realistic verse that portrayed ordinary people in every day situations. Frost was the recipient of the Pulitzer Prize a remarkable four times.

Alice Fulton is the author of several books of poetry, including *Palladium*, winner of the 1985 National Poetry Award. Her work has appeared in five editions of the *Best American Poetry* book series.

Kahlil Gibran (1883–1931) was a Syrian-American philosophical essayist, novelist, and poet. A deeply religious man, Gibran wrote work that is highly romantic in outlook, and was greatly influenced by William Blake, Nietzsche, and the Bible.

Garbage emerged from an informal jam session between producers Butch Vig, Steve Maker, and Duke Erikson. The trio later recruited former *Angelfish* vocalist, Shirley Manson. The band went on to record two hit albums and performed the title song for the 1999 James Bond film, *The World Is Not Enough*.

Allen Ginsberg (1926–97) was a Beat poet, as well as a dedicated antiwar activist and spokesman for the counterculture. He published more than forty books of poetry.

Macy Gray began singing while studying screen writing at the University of Southern California, recording a demo with friends after the scheduled vocalist failed to show up at the studio. Her debut album, *On How Life Is*, was released in 1999.

Thomas Hardy (1840–1928), trained architect, English novelist and poet, set much of his work in Wessex, an imaginary county in southwestern England. His books, among them *Tess of the D'urbervilles* and *Jude the Obscure*, are considered literary classics today.

Beth Hart is a Los Angeles-based blues-rocker who began playing the piano at age four. She later attended L.A.'s High School for the Performing Arts as a vocal and cello major. The Beth Hart Band released its debut album, *Immortal*, in 1996.

Jimi Hendrix (1942-1970), American rock guitarist, singer, and composer, fused American traditions of blues, jazz, rock, and soul with techniques of British avant-garde rock to completely redefine the electric guitar in his own image.

Hermann Hesse (1877–1962), German novelist, poet, and literary critic, was most concerned with exploring man's spiritual loneliness in such books as *Steppenwolf*. He was awarded the Nobel Prize for literature in 1946.

Hole is fronted by rock-star-turned-Hollywood-actress Courtney Love. Four days before the release of the band's highly successful 1994 album, *Live Through This*, Love's husband and former Nirvana front man, Kurt Cobain, was found dead of a self-inflicted gunshot wound. The band released their third full-length album, *Celebrity Skin*, in 1998.

Horace (65 BC–8 BC) was an outstanding Latin lyric poet and satirist under the emperor Augustus of Rome.

A. E. Housman (1859–1936), English poet and classical scholar, is best known for his poetry collection *A Shropshire Lad*.

Jewel is a singer, songwriter, published poet, and film actress. Raised in remote Homer, Alaska, she began her music career at the age of six, performing alongside her parents in Eskimo villages and tourist attractions. Ever since her 1995 debut album, *Pieces of You*, Jewel's folk-inspired ballads have topped music charts.

Rickie Lee Jones has been touted as the natural successor to Joni Mitchell throughout her career as a singer-songwriter. She worked a series of waitressing jobs while occasionally performing in Los Angeles nightclubs, where she honed her unique, Beat-influenced spoken-word monologues and songwriting.

John Keats (1795–1821), English romantic lyric poet, devoted his short, tragic life to the perfection of a poetry marked by great sensual appeal, vivid imagery, and an attempt to express a philosophy through classical legend.

John Lennon (1940-1980) was a founding member of the most celebrated rock band in history, The Beatles. Just as his roller coaster solo career was on the upswing, Lennon was tragically assassinated outside of his New York City apartment building. He left behind an enormous legacy, not only as a musician, but as an artist, writer, actor, and activist.

Beth Lisick is one of the few slam poets to be featured in *The Best American Poetry 1997*, edited by James Tate. She is the author of *Monkey Girl*, a collection of West Coast narratives.

Amy Lowell (1874–1925) was an American critic and lecturer and a leading poet of the Imagist school. "Lilacs" and "Patterns" are among her most frequently anthologized works.

Aimee Mann led the post-new wave group, 'Til Tuesday, during the 1980s. Her solo recording career has been plagued by record company problems and disputes, but she was nominated for an Oscar in 2000 for a song from the soundtrack to the film, *Magnolia*.

Douglas A. Martin is the author of a novel, *Outline of My Lover*, and two books of poetry, *Servicing the Salamander* and *My Gradual Demise & Honeysuckle*, and co-author of *The Haiku Year*. His work is included in the anthologies *Best Gay Erotica 2000* and *Latin Lovers*.

Jeffrey McDaniel is the author of *Alibi School* and *The Forgiveness Parade*. His work appeared in *Best American Poetry 1996*. He currently writes reviews and literary interviews for *CUPS* magazine in Los Angeles.

Michelangelo (1475–1564), Italian Renaissance sculptor, painter, architect, and poet, exerted an unparalleled influence on the development of Western art. Michelangelo was considered the greatest living artist in his lifetime. He was the first artist to have his biography published while he was still alive.

Edna St. Vincent Millay (1892-1950), bisexual American poet and dramatist, came to personify romantic rebellion and bravado in the 1920s. For a time she supported herself in New York City by writing short stories and plays under the pseudonym Nancy Boyd.

A. A. Milne (1882–1956) is best remembered for creating the children's classic *Winnie-the-Pooh*. His son, Christopher Robin, and his toy bear, pig, donkey, tiger, and kangaroo were the inspiration for the book.

Marianne Moore (1887–1972), American poet, won the admiration of her fellow poets throughout her long career. Her best-known work includes "Poetry"—which was the source of her often quoted admonition that poets should present imaginary gardens with real toads in them.

Pablo Neruda (1904–73), Chilean diplomat, politician, and one of the most important Latin-American poets of the twentieth century, was awarded the Nobel Prize for literature in 1971.

Friedrich Nietzsche (1844–1900), German classical scholar, philosopher, and cultural critic, was one of the most influential of all modern thinkers. His works greatly affected generations of theologians, poets, novelists, and scholars.

Notorious B.I.G. (1972-1997), born Chris Wallace, emerged as the most visible figure in East Coast hip-hop in the mid-1990s. With the success of his 1995 debut album, *Ready to Die*,

Notorious B.I.G. became a target in the heated rivalry between rappers from the two coasts. In 1997, Notorious B.I.G. was gunned down outside of a Los Angeles hotel. His posthumous second album, *Life After Death*, debuted at number one on the record charts.

Frank O'Hara (1926–66), American poet, gathered images from the urban environment to represent his own personal experiences. He was drawn to both poetry and the visual arts and during the 1960s was the assistant curator at the Museum of Modern Art in New York City. His poetry is a dizzying mixture of quotes, phone numbers, commercials, and gossip.

Mary Oliver is a winner of the National Book Award and the Pulitzer Prize. Her books include *American Primitive*, *Dream Work*, and *Twelve Moons*. She has conducted poetry workshops at colleges and universities throughout the country.

112 is the first and most successful urban vocal group to emerge from Sean "Puffy" Combs' Bad Boys Records roster. The quartet met each other while attending high school in Atlanta, Georgia. They released *Room 112* in 1998.

Ishle Yi Park is a spoken-word poet who has performed at numerous venues on the East Coast. She is a poetry editor for the *Asian Pacific American Journal*, a writing teacher for CreateNow, a workshop geared toward Asian American youth, and teaches writing workshops at a women's prison. Her work has been published in various journals and anthologies including *New American Writing* and *The NuyorAsian Anthology: Asian American Writings about New York City*.

Octavio Paz (1914–98), Mexican poet, writer, and diplomat, was recognized as a major literary figure in Latin America after World War II. Paz, whose family grew up destitute, turned to writing and at the age of nineteen, published his first book of poetry, *Luna Silvestre*. He received the Nobel Prize for literature in 1990.

Liz Phair rocketed from modest homemade recording projects to national stardom in the spring of 1993 with the release of her debut album, *Exile in Guyville*. Phair became the figurehead for a new generation of female alternative rock musicians.

Pink Floyd was a British rock band at the forefront of 1960s psychedelia. Their 1973 album, *Dark Side of the Moon*, spent an incomprehensible 741 weeks on the Billboard album charts, cementing its place among the most popular rock albums of all time.

Sylvia Plath (1932–63) was an American poet and novelist whose best-known works, including *The Bell Jar*, are noted for their preoccupation with alienation, death, and despair. Though still an unknown when she took her own life, Plath's reputation and popularity grew posthumously, and by the mid-1970s she was considered a major contemporary poet.

Alexander Pope (1688–1744) was a poet and satirist of the English Augustan period. He is generally considered one of the most quotable of all English authors.

Jerry Quickley, a slam poet, is a three-time Los Angeles Grand Slam winner and a two-time National Slam finalist. Jerry also performs on the new CD *Unbound* with Pharaoh Monche, Zach de la Rocha, Ursula

Rucker, Saul Williams, and other hip-hop and spoken-word artists. Jerry runs a Poetry in the Prisons workshop at Central Juvenile Hall in Los Angeles.
Radiohead, alternative rock band, was pigeonholed as a one hit wonder based on 1993's hit single "Creep", but the band won widespread acclaim for 1995's *The Bends* and 1997's *OK Computer*.
Rainer Maria Rilke (1875–1926), Austro-German poet, became internationally famous for such works as *Duino Elegies* and *Sonnets to Orpheus*.
Ed Roland is the lead vocalist/guitarist/songwriter of the band Collective Soul. He formed the band in the mid-1980s after dropping out of music school. Roland's parents did not allow him to listen to music as a child.
J. D. Salinger is a renowned writer who established his reputation on the basis of a single novel, *The Catcher in the Rye*. Known as a recluse, Salinger left New York City for the wooded hills of New Hampshire due to the public attention he received after the novel was published.
William Shakespeare (1564–1616) was an English dramatist, poet, and actor. Often called the English national poet, Shakespeare is considered the greatest dramatist of all time.
Percy Bysshe Shelley (1792-1822) was an English romantic poet whose work reflected his revolutionary political idealism and his strong faith in the spiritual power of the imagination. He drowned in a boating accident in Italy, where he had settled with his second wife, Mary Wollstonecraft Shelley, the author of *Frankenstein*.
Beau Sia is an artist whose credits include a CD entitled *Attack! Attack! Go!*, a book of poetry entitled *A Night Without Armor II: The Revenge*, appearances in the films *Slam* and *Slam Nation*, and work featured in the anthologies *Poetry Nation*, *Heights of the Marvelous*, and *Everybody Wants a Boy*. He began writing because of a girl he loved.
Charles Simic, born in Yugoslavia, evokes his Eastern European heritage and his childhood experiences during World War II to comment poetically on the scarcity of spirituality in contemporary life.
Robert Louis Stevenson (1850–94), Scottish essayist, poet, and author, is best known for his novels *Treasure Island*, *Kidnapped*, and *Dr. Jekyll and Mr. Hyde*.
Dylan Thomas (1914–53) was a Welsh poet and prose writer whose work is known for its comic exuberance and intense lyricism. His first book, *18 Poems*, was published when he was twenty. His reading tours of the United States did much to popularize poetry reading as a new medium of art. Thomas died from alcoholism at the age of thirty-nine.
Rob Thomas is the lead singer and lyricist of the rock band Matchbox Twenty. The band's debut album, *Yourself or Someone Like You*, achieved gold status. Thomas collaborated with Carlos Santana on the Grammy award-winning 1999 Santana album, *Supernatural*.
TLC is a Georgia-based hip-hop trio who released their first album, *Ooooooohhh . . . on the TLC Tip*, in 1992. *CrazySexyCool*, released in 1994, featured three number-one singles and sold over four million copies. The trio released their third record,

Fan Mail, in 1999.

Lionel Trilling (1905–75) was an American literary critic and teacher whose criticism was informed by psychological, sociological, and philosophical methods and insights.

Virgil (70 BC–19 BC), the greatest Roman poet of all time, was best known for his epic *The Aeneid*.

Tom Waits is a singer-songwriter with a distinctive, gravelly voice. He is one of rock's most uncompromising individualists, and a talented comic actor.

Simone Weil (1909–43), French mystic, social philosopher, and activist in the French Resistance during World War II, was referred to as the saint of all outsiders.

Walt Whitman (1819–92), American poet, journalist, and essayist, was the inventor of modern free verse, and his influence has been—and continues to be—incalculable. Whitman, who had no schooling beyond the age of thirteen, self-published his verse collection, *Leaves of Grass*, in 1855. It remains a landmark in the history of American literature.

Oscar Wilde (1854–1900), Irish poet, wit, and dramatist, was the spokesman for the late-nineteenth-century aesthetic movement in England. Wilde is best known for his comic masterpieces *Lady Windermere's Fan* and *The Importance of Being Earnest*. He was also the object of a controversial civil and criminal trial involving homosexuality that ended in his imprisonment.

Saul Williams, slam poet and spoken word recording artist cowrote and starred in the award-winning 1998 independent film *Slam*. Williams is also the author of the poetry collections *S^he* and *The Seventh Octave*.

William Carlos Williams (1883–1963), American poet, succeeded in making the ordinary appear extraordinary through the clarity and directness of his imagery. Williams, a practicing physician, juggled a life of poetry and medicine in his hometown of Rutherford, New Jersey.

credits

"Dominican Girdles," by Dana Bryant. © Dana Bryant.

"Flowin' Prose" words and music by Michael Diamond, Adam Horovitz, Adam N. Yauch and Mario Caldato, Jr. © 1998 Universal-Polygram International Publishing, Inc., a division of Universal Studios, Inc. (ASCAP). International copyright secured. All rights reserved.

"Foolish Games" by Jewel Kilcher. © 1995 WB Music Corp. and Wiggly Tooth Music. All rights administered by WB Music Corp. All rights reserved. Used by permission.

"For the Mad," first published in *two-headed woman,* © 1980 by The University of Massachusetts Press, published by The University of Massachusetts Press. Now appears in *good woman*, © 1987 by Lucille Clifton, published by Boa Editions, Ltd. Reprinted by permission of Curtis Brown, Ltd.

"Girl's Room" by Liz Phair. © Sony/ATV Tunes LLC. All rights reserved.

"Ghost World" by Aimee Mann. © 1999 Aimee Mann. All rights reserved.

"Hands" by Jewel Kilcher and Patrick Leonard. © 1998 WB Music Corp., Wiggly Tooth Music and Bumyamaki Music. All rights on behalf of Wiggly Tooth Music administered by WB Music Corp. All rights on behalf of Bumyamaki Music administered by Wixen Music Publishing, Inc. All rights reserved. Used by permission.

"Heaven Tonight" by Courtney Love. © Mother May I Music. Lyrics used with permission of Cherry Lane Music Publishing on behalf of the publisher. All rights reserved.

"Howl," by Beau Sia. © 2000 Beau Sia.

"Isobel" by Bjork, Nellee Hooper, Maurice De Vires, and Sjon. © Famous Music Publishing, Warner Chappell Music, 19 Music, BMG Music and Copyright Control. All rights reserved.

"It's Cold Outside," by Felice Belle. © Felice Belle.

"It Takes A Lot To Laugh It Takes A Train to Cry" by Bob Dylan. © Special Rider Music. All rights reserved.

"Joyful Girl" by Ani DiFranco. © 1996 Righteous Babe Music (BMI). Used with permission. All rights reserved.

"Love," by Beau Sia. © 2000 Beau Sia.

"Love Song For The Drummer," by Dot Antoniades. © 1999 Dot Antoniades.

"Love Sonnet XIV", © Pablo Neruda, 1959 and Heirs of Pablo Neruda. © 1986 by the University of Texas Press. All rights reserved. Originally published as *Cien sonetos de amor*. © Editorial Losada, S.A., Buenos Aires, 1960. Reprinted by permission.

"Me" by Paula Cole. © Ensign Music. Lyrics used with permission of Famous Music Publishing on behalf of the publisher. All rights reserved.

"Moonchild" by Cibo Matto. © Soul Urchin Songs. All rights reserved.

"My Life" by Roy Ayers, Mary J. Blige, Sean "Puffy" Combs, and Arlene Del Valle. © Chrysalis Music, EMI April Music, Inc., Jelly's Jams LLC, and Universal MCA Music Publishing. All rights reserved.

"no surprises" by Colin Greenwood, Jonathan Greenwood, Edward O'Brien, Philip Selway, and Thomas Yorke. © Warner Chappell Music, Inc. All rights reserved.

"Peer," by Douglas A. Martin. In *Servicing The Salamander*. Champion Books. © 1998 Douglas A. Martin. Reprinted by permission of the author.

"Phenomenal Woman," from *And Still I Rise* by Maya Angelou, © 1978 by Maya Angelou. Reprinted by permission of Random House, Inc. (U.S.) and Little, Brown (U.K.).

"Plugging the Basketball Diaries . . . ," by Regie Cabico. © Regie Cabico.

"Pocahontas Grants An Interview . . ." by Regie Cabico. In Will Work For Peace. © 1999 Regie Cabico. Reprinted by permission of the author.

"Purple Haze" by Jimi Hendrix. © Experience Hendrix LLC. All rights reserved.

"Sea Features," by Jerry Quickley. © Jerry Quickley.

"Sky's The Limit" by Caldwell Robert Hunter, Sean "Puffy" Combs, DJ Clark Kent, Hubert B. Eaves, III, Christopher Wallace, and James N. Williams. © Blue Image Music, Clark S. True Funk Music, EMI Longitude Music, The Music Force, Zella Music, and EMI April Music. All rights reserved.

"somewhere i have never travelled,gladly beyond." Copyright 1931, © 1959, 1991 by the Trustees for the E. E. Cummings Trust. © 1979 by George James Firmage, from *Complete Poems: 1904-1962* by E. E. Cummings, edited by George J. Firmage. Used by permission of Liveright Publishing Corporation.

"The Day Lady Died," from *Lunch Poems*. © 1960 by Frank O'Hara. Reprinted by permission of City Lights Books.

"The Geography of My Body," by Ishle Yi Park. Title inspired by "Geography of My Face" by Khaled Mattawa. © Ishle Yi Park.

"The Quiet World," by Jeffrey McDaniel. In *The Forgiveness Parade*. Manic D Press. © 1998 Jeffrey McDaniel. Reprinted with permission of the publisher and author.

"Things To Do In Saratoga When You're Bored," by Beth Lisick. In *Monkey Girl*. Manic D Press. © 1997 Beth Lisick. Reprinted with permission of the publisher and author.

"Third Stone From The Sun," by Jimi Hendrix. © Experience Hendrix LLC. All rights reserved.

"This Is Just to Say" and "The Red Wheelbarrow," by William Carlos Williams, from *Collected Poems: 1909-1939*, Volume I, © 1938 by New Directions Publishing Corp, Reprinted by permission of New Directions Publishing Corp. (U.S.) and Carcanet Press Limited (U.K.).

"tropicalia" by Beck Hansen. © BMG Songs. All rights reserved.

"Try To Pretend," by Cheryl B. In the chapbook *New York Girl*. Vanishing Point Press, 2000. © 2000 Cheryl B.

"Unpretty" by Dallas Austin and Tionne Watkins. © EMI April Music. All rights reserved.

"We Real Cool," first published in *The Bean Eaters* by Gwendolyn Brooks. © 1960 Gwendolyn Brooks Blakely. All rights reserved. No part of this poem may be reproduced, stored in a retrieval system or transmitted in any form, by any means, including mechanical, electronic, photocopying, recording, or otherwise, without prior written permission of the author. Reprinted by permission of Gwendolyn Brooks Blakely.

"Why I Am Not a Painter," from *Collected Poems by Frank O'Hara*, © 1958 by Maureen Granville-Smith, Administratrix of the Estate of Frank O'Hara. Reprinted by permission of Alfred A. Knopf, a Division of Random House, Inc.

"Wildish," by Douglas A. Martin. © Douglas A. Martin.

"You Come Back," from *Morning in the Burned House* by Margaret Atwood, © 1995 by Margaret Atwood. Reprinted by permission of Houghton Mifflin Co. (U.S.) and Curtis Brown, Ltd. (U.K.). All rights reserved.

Acknowledgments:

Thanks to Julie Agrati, Dr. Edison Amos, Farshid Arshid, Cathy Carapella, Ann Christophe, Laura Ciocia, Patti Conte, Mauro DePreta, Vicky Germaise, David Hunt, Jason Kurtz, Michael Lippman, Karen Mason, Tom Mellers, Andrea Moss, Mona Scott, Jodi Smith, Arthur Spivak, Eben Weiss, John Witherspoon, David Wolff.

Special thanks to all the poets for their time, work, and enthusiasm.

Photograph credits:

Austin, Kim, 76; Ekert, Ralf, 82, 101, 102, 114, 136; Gordon, Russell, 15; Haynes, Loren, 4; Kleinberger, Dawn, 60; Kirschen, Alan, 67; Lane, Colin, 80; McCusker, Elspeth, 65, 88; Monchik, Lauren, 20, 32, 43, 44, 71, 86, 89, 99, 110, 116, 129, 135, 144; Papazain, Ellen, 19, 34; Photodisc, 40, 69; Vengoechea, Paola, 11, 12, 63, 96, 132.